Applied Neural Networks with TensorFlow 2

API Oriented Deep Learning with Python

Orhan Gazi Yalçın

Apress®

*Applied Neural Networks with TensorFlow 2: API Oriented Deep
Learning with Python*

Orhan Gazi Yalçın
Istanbul, Turkey

ISBN-13 (pbk): 978-1-4842-6512-3   ISBN-13 (electronic): 978-1-4842-6513-0
https://doi.org/10.1007/978-1-4842-6513-0

Managing Director, Apress Media LLC: Welmoed Spahr
Acquisitions Editor: Aaron Black
Development Editor: James Markham
Coordinating Editor: Jessica Vakili

Distributed to the book trade worldwide by Springer Science+Business Media New York,1
NY Plazar, New York, NY 10014. Phone 1-800-SPRINGER, fax (201) 348-4505, e-mail
orders-ny@springer-sbm.com, or visit www.springeronline.com. Apress Media, LLC is a
California LLC and the sole member (owner) is Springer Science + Business Media Finance
Inc (SSBM Finance Inc). SSBM Finance Inc is a **Delaware** corporation.

For information on translations, please e-mail booktranslations@springernature.com; for
reprint, paperback, or audio rights, please e-mail bookpermissions@springernature.com.

Apress titles may be purchased in bulk for academic, corporate, or promotional use. eBook
versions and licenses are also available for most titles. For more information, reference our
Print and eBook Bulk Sales web page at http://www.apress.com/bulk-sales.

Any source code or other supplementary material referenced by the author in this book is
available to readers on GitHub via the book's product page, located at www.apress.com/
978-1-4842-6512-3. For more detailed information, please visit http://www.apress.com/
source-code.

Printed on acid-free paper

I dedicate this book to my overcurious dad, Lutfi – who kept sneaking into the study room to see how far I was into the book – and to my mom, Ayşe, for always supporting and encouraging me.

I would also like to thank my friend, Enes, for encouraging me to write this book in the first place.

Finally, I would like to thank my sister and brother, Merve and Kürşat, and all my friends who supported me throughout the whole process – all the way – till the last word.

Table of Contents

About the Author

Orhan Gazi Yalçın is a joint PhD candidate at the University of Bologna and the Polytechnic University of Madrid. After completing his double major in business and law, he began his career in Istanbul, working for a city law firm, Allen & Overy, and a global entrepreneurship network, Endeavor. During his academic and professional career, he taught himself programming and excelled in machine learning. He currently conducts research on hotly debated law and AI topics such as explainable artificial intelligence and the right to explanation by combining his technical and legal skills. In his spare time, he enjoys free diving, swimming, exercising, as well as discovering new countries, cultures, and cuisines.

- You can visit Orhan's personal web page at

  www.orhangaziyalcin.com

- Also feel free to connect with Orhan on Linkedin at

  www.linkedin.com/in/orhangaziyalcin

About the Technical Reviewer

Vishwesh Ravi Shrimali graduated from BITS Pilani in 2018, where he studied mechanical engineering. Since then, he has worked with BigVision LLC on deep learning and computer vision and was involved in creating official OpenCV AI courses. Currently, he is working at Mercedes Benz Research and Development India Pvt. Ltd. He has a keen interest in programming and AI and has applied that interest in mechanical engineering projects. He has also written multiple blogs on OpenCV and deep learning on LearnOpenCV, a leading blog on computer vision. He has also coauthored *Machine Learning for OpenCV4* (second edition) by Packt. When he is not writing blogs or working on projects, he likes to go on long walks or play his acoustic guitar.

Acknowledgments

This book was written during a global lockdown due to the Covid-19 pandemic, which created a new normal that I have never experienced before. Writing a book in the middle of a global crisis was a very intense experience, and I was uncertain about taking this responsibility for a long time. Thanks to my family and friends, I was able to complete the book even earlier than scheduled. Now I am glad that I accepted Aaron's invitation, who guided me throughout the whole process. Thank you very much for reaching out to me in the first place and making it possible to have this book written.

I would like to thank Jessica Vakili for coordinating the entire project and for being there whenever I needed. I would also like to thank Vishwesh Ravi Shrimali for reviewing every single line of the book and providing me with all the valuable comments, which helped to improve the quality of the book tremendously.

Being surrounded with people who all have a positive attitude made this experience very fruitful, and I am looking forward to working with them in the future. Thank you all very much!

CHAPTER 1

Introduction

In this book, we dive into the realms of deep learning (DL) and cover several deep learning concepts along with several case studies. These case studies range from image recognition to recommender systems, from art generation to object clustering. Deep learning is part of a broader family of machine learning (ML) methods based on **artificial neural networks (ANNs)** with representation learning. These neural networks mimic the human brain cells, or neurons, for algorithmic learning, and their learning speed is much faster than human learning speed. Several deep learning methods offer solutions to different types of machine learning problems: (i) supervised learning, (ii) unsupervised learning, (iii) semi-supervised learning, and (iv) reinforcement learning.

This book is structured in a way to also include an introduction to the discipline of machine learning so that the reader may be acquainted with the general rules and concepts of machine learning. Then, a detailed introduction to deep learning is provided to familiarize the reader with the sub-discipline of deep learning.

After covering the fundamentals of deep learning, the book covers different types of artificial neural networks with their potential real-life applications (i.e., case studies). Therefore, at each chapter, this book (i) introduces the concept of a particular neural network architecture with details on its components and then (ii) provides a tutorial on how to apply this network structure to solve a particular artificial intelligence (AI) problem.

© Orhan Gazi Yalçın 2021
O. G. Yalçın, *Applied Neural Networks with TensorFlow 2,*
https://doi.org/10.1007/978-1-4842-6513-0_1

Since the goal of this book is to provide case studies for deep learning applications, the competency in several technologies and libraries is sought for a satisfactory learning experience.

Before diving into machine learning and deep learning, we start with the introduction to the technologies used in this book. This introduction includes the latest developments and the reasoning as to why these technologies are selected. Finally, this chapter also covers how to install these technologies and prepare your environment with a minimum amount of hassle. The technologies that are in the center of this book are as follows:

- Our Selected Programming Language: **Python 3.x**

- Our Selected Deep Learning Framework: **TensorFlow 2.x**

- Our Development Environment: **Google Colab** (*with Jupyter Notebook alternative*)

Note A TensorFlow Pipeline Guide showing how to use TensorFlow can be found in Chapter 5, whereas the relevant libraries used with TensorFlow are covered in Chapter 4.

Please note that this book assumes that you use Google Colab, which requires almost no environment setup. The chapter also includes a local Jupyter Notebook installation guide if you prefer a local environment. You may skip the Jupyter Notebook installation section if you decide to use Google Colab.

Note When learning a new programming discipline or technology, one of the most demoralizing tasks is the environment setup process. Therefore, it is important to simplify this process as much as possible. Therefore, this chapter is designed with this principle in mind.

Python as Programming Language

Python is a programming language created by Guido van Rossum as a side project and was initially released in 1991. Python supports object-oriented programming (OOP), a paradigm based on the concept of objects, which can contain data, in the form of fields. Python prioritizes the programmer's experience. Therefore, programmers can write clear and logical code for both small and large projects. It also contains support for functional programming. Python is dynamically typed and garbage collected.

Python is also considered as an interpreted language because it goes through an interpreter, which turns code you write into the language understood by your computer's processor. An interpreter executes the statements of code "one by one." On the other hand, in compiled languages, a compiler executes the code entirely and lists all possible errors at a time. The compiled code is more efficient than the interpreted code in terms of speed and performance. However, scripted languages such as Python show only one error message even though your code has multiple errors. This feature helps the programmer to clear errors quickly, and it increases the development speed.

Timeline of Python

Let's take a look at the timeline of Python:

- In the late 1980s, Python was conceived as a successor to the ABC language.

- In December 1989, Guido van Rossum started Python's implementation.

- In January 1994, Python version 1.0 was released. The major new features included were the functional programming tools lambda, map, filter, and reduce.

- October 2000, Python 2.0 was released with major new features, including a cycle-detecting garbage collector and support for Unicode.

- Python 3.0 was released on December 3, 2008. It was a major revision of the language that is only partially backward compatible. Many of its major features were backported to Python 2.6.x and 2.7.x version series. Releases of Python 3 include the 2 to 3 utility, which automates (at least partially) the translation of Python 2 code to Python 3.

- As of January 1, 2020, no new bug reports, fixes, or changes are made to Python 2, and **Python 2 is no longer supported**.

Python 2 vs. Python 3

One of the common questions a new deep learning programmer might have is whether to use Python 2.x or Python 3.x since there are many outdated blog posts and web articles comparing two major versions. As of 2020, it is safe to claim that these comparisons are not relevant. As you may see in the preceding timeline, the delayed deprecation of Python 2.x finally took place as of January 1, 2020. Therefore, programmers may not find official support for Python 2.x versions anymore.

One of the essential skills for a programmer is to be up to date with the latest technology, and therefore, this book only utilizes the use of Python 3.x versions. For the readers who are only familiar with Python 2.x versions, this preference should not pose a problem since the differences between the syntax used in this book for Python 2.x and Python 3.x are not significant. Therefore, Python 2.x programmers may immediately familiarize themselves with the source code in this book.

Why Python?

Compared to other programming languages, there are several reasons for Python's popularity among data scientists and machine learning engineers. 2019 Kaggle Machine Learning and Data Science Survey revealed that Python is by far the most popular programming language for data science and machine learning; see Figure 1-1.

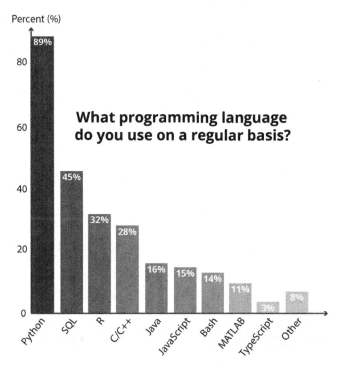

Figure 1-1. *2019 Kaggle Machine Learning and Data Science Survey*

There are several reasons for Python's popularity compared to other languages. A non-exhaustive list of benefits of Python may be the following.

Ease of Learning

One of the main reasons for newcomers to choose Python as their primary programming language is its ease of learning. When compared to other programming languages, Python offers a shorter learning curve so that programmers can achieve a good level of competency in a short amount of time. Python's syntax is easier to learn, and the code is more readable compared to other popular programming languages. A common example to show this is the amount of code required by different programming languages to print out "Hello, World!". For instance, to be able to print out Hello, World! in Java, you need the following code:

Hello, World! In Java

```java
public class Main {
    public static void main(String[] args) {
        System.out.println("Hello, World!");
    }
}
```

The same result may be achieved with a single line of code in Python:

```python
Hello, World! in Python
print("Hello, World!")
```

A Variety of Available Data Science Libraries

Another powerful characteristic of Python compared to other programming languages is its wide variety of data science libraries. The data science libraries such as Pandas, NumPy, SciPy, and scikit-learn reduce the time to prepare the data for model training with their standardized functions and modules for logical and mathematical operations. Furthermore, thanks to the vibrant community of Python developers, as soon as the developers detect a common problem, a new library is immediately designed and released to address this problem.

Community Support

The powerful community support is another advantage of Python over other programming languages. More and more volunteers are releasing Python libraries, and this practice made Python the language with modern and powerful libraries. Besides, a high number of seasoned Python programmers are always ready to help other programmers with their problems on online community channels such as Stack Overflow.

Visualization Options

Data visualization is an important discipline to extract insights from raw data, and Python offers several useful visualization options. The good old Matplotlib is always there with the most customizable options. In addition, Seaborn and Pandas Plot API are powerful libraries that streamline the most common visualization tasks used by data scientists. Additionally, libraries like Plotly and Dash allow users to create interactive plots and sophisticated dashboards to be served on the Web. With these libraries, data scientists may easily create charts, draw graphical plots, and facilitate feature extraction.

Now that we covered why favorite language of data scientists is Python, we can move on to why we use TensorFlow as our machine learning framework.

TensorFlow As Deep Learning Framework

TensorFlow TensorFlow is an open source machine learning platform with a particular focus on neural networks, developed by the Google Brain team. Despite initially being used for internal purposes,

Google released the library under the Apache License 2.0 in November 2015, which made it an open source library.[1] Although the use cases of TensorFlow are not limited to machine learning applications, machine learning is the field where we see TensorFlow's strength.

The two programming languages with stable and official TensorFlow APIs are Python and C. Also, C++, Java, JavaScript, Go, and Swift are other programming languages where developers may find limited-to-extensive TensorFlow compatibility. Finally, there are third-party TensorFlow APIs for C#, Haskell, Julia, MATLAB, R, Scala, Rust, OCaml, and Crystal.

Timeline of TensorFlow

Although this book focuses on TensorFlow 2.x with Python API, there are several complementary TensorFlow libraries released by Google. Understanding the development of the TensorFlow platform is essential to see the full picture. The timeline of the milestones achieved by Google as part of the TensorFlow project may be summarized as follows:

- In 2011, Google Brain built a machine learning system called **DistBelief** using deep learning neural networks.

- November 2015, Google released the TensorFlow library under the Apache License 2.0 and made it **open source** to accelerate the advancements in artificial intelligence.

---

[1] Google Just Open Sourced TensorFlow, Its Artificial Intelligence Engine | WIRED, www.wired.com/2015/11/google-open-sources-its-artificial-intelligence-engine/ (last visited Jun 5, 2020)

- In May 2016, Google announced an application-specific integrated circuit (an ASIC) built for machine learning and tailored for TensorFlow, called **Tensor Processing Unit (TPU)**.

- In February 2017, Google released **TensorFlow 1.0.0.**

- In May 2017, Google announced **TensorFlow Lite,** a library for machine learning development in mobile devices.

- In December 2017, Google introduced **Kubeflow**, which allows operation and deployment of TensorFlow on Kubernetes.

- In March 2018, Google announced **TensorFlow.js** version 1.0 for machine learning with JavaScript.

- In July 2018, Google announced the **Edge TPU**. Edge TPU is Google's purpose-built ASIC chip designed to run TensorFlow Lite machine learning (ML) models on smartphones.

- In January 2019, Google announced **TensorFlow 2.0** to be officially available in September 2019.

- In May 2019, Google announced **TensorFlow Graphics** for deep learning in computer graphics.

- In September 2019, TensorFlow Team released **TensorFlow 2.0**, a new major version of the library.

This timeline shows that the TensorFlow platform is maturing. Especially with the release of TensorFlow 2.0, Google has improved the user-friendliness of TensorFlow APIs significantly. Besides, the TensorFlow team announced that they don't intend to introduce any other significant changes. Therefore, it is safe to assume that the methods and syntax included in this book are to keep their relevance for a long time.

Why TensorFlow?

There are more than two dozens of deep learning libraries developed by tech giants, tech foundations, and academic institutions that are available to the public. While each framework has its advantage in a particular sub-discipline of deep learning, this book focuses on TensorFlow with Keras API. The main reason for choosing TensorFlow over other deep learning frameworks is its popularity. On the other hand, this statement does not indicate that the other frameworks are better – yet, less popular – than TensorFlow. Especially with the introduction of version 2.0, TensorFlow strengthened its power by addressing the issues raised by the deep learning community. Today, TensorFlow may be seen as the most popular deep learning framework, which is very powerful and easy to use and has excellent community support.

What's New in TensorFlow 2.x

Since its introduction in 2015, TensorFlow has grown into one of the most advanced machine learning platforms in the market. Researchers, developers, and companies widely adopted the technologies introduced by the TensorFlow team. Around its 4th birthday, TensorFlow 2.0 was released in September 2019. The TensorFlow team put a lot of effort into simplifying the APIs by cleaning up deprecated APIs and reducing duplication. The TensorFlow team introduced several updates to achieve simplicity and ease of use in TensorFlow 2.0. These updates may be listed as follows:

1. Easy model building with Keras and eager execution

2. Robust model deployment in production level on any platform

3. Robust experimentation for research

4. Simplified API thanks to cleanups and duplication reduction

Easy Model Building with Keras and Eager Execution

The TensorFlow team further streamlined the model building experience to respond to expectations with the new or improved modules such as tf.data, tf.keras, and tf.estimators and the Distribution Strategy API.

Load Your Data Using tf.data

In TensorFlow 2.0, training data is read using input pipelines created with the tf.data module. tf.feature_column module is used to define feature characteristics. What is useful for newcomers is the new DataSets module. TensorFlow 2.0 offers a separate DataSets module which offers a range of popular datasets and allows developers to experiment with these datasets.

Build, Train, and Validate Your Model with tf.keras, or Use Premade Estimators

In TensorFlow 1.x, developers could use the previous versions of tf.contrib, tf.layers, tf.keras, and tf.estimators to build models. Offering four different options to the same problem confused the newcomers and drove some of them away, especially to PyTorch. TensorFlow 2.0 simplified the model building by limiting the options to two improved modules: tf.keras (TensorFlow Keras API) and tf.estimators (Estimator API). TensorFlow Keras API offers a high-level interface that makes model building easy, which is especially useful for *proof of concepts (POC)*. On the other hand, Estimator API is better suited for production-level models that require scaled serving and increased customization capability.

Run and Debug with Eager Execution, Then Use AutoGraph API for the Benefits of Graphs

TensorFlow 1.x versions were prioritizing TensorFlow graphs, which is not friendly to newcomers. Even though this complicated methodology was kept in TensorFlow 2.0, eager execution – the contrast concept – was made default. Google explained the initial reasoning for this change with the following statement:

> *Eager execution is an imperative, define-by-run interface where operations are executed immediately as they are called from Python. This makes it easier to get started with TensorFlow, and can make research and development more intuitive.*[2]

Eager execution makes the model building easier. It offers fast debugging capability with immediate runtime errors and integration with Python tools, which makes TensorFlow more beginner friendly. On the other hand, graph execution has advantages for distributed training, performance optimizations, and production deployment. To fill this gap, TensorFlow introduced AutoGraph API called via `tf.function` decorator. This book prioritizes eager execution over graph execution to achieve a steep learning curve for the reader.

Use Distribution Strategies for Distributed Training

Model training with large datasets necessitates distributed training with multiple processors such as CPU, GPU, or TPU. Even though TensorFlow 1.x has support for distributed training, Distribution Strategy API optimizes and streamlines the distributed training across multiple GPUs, multiple

---

[2]Google AI Blog: Eager Execution: An imperative, define-by-run interface to TensorFlow, https://ai.googleblog.com/2017/10/eager-execution-imperative-define-by.html (last visited Jun 8, 2020)

machines, or TPUs. TensorFlow also provides templates to deploy training on Kubernetes clusters in on-prem or cloud environments, which makes the training more cost-effective.

Export to SavedModel

After training a model, developers may export to SavedModel. `tf.saved_model` API may be used to build a complete TensorFlow program with weights and computations. This standardized SavedModel can be used interchangeably across different TensorFlow deployment libraries such as (i) TensorFlow Serving, (ii) TensorFlow Lite, (iii) TensorFlow.js, and (iv) TensorFlow Hub.

Robust Model Deployment in Production on Any Platform

TensorFlow has always made efforts to provide a direct path to production on different devices. There are already several libraries which may be used to serve the trained models on dedicated environments.

TensorFlow Serving

TensorFlow Serving is a flexible and high-performance TensorFlow library that allows models to be served over HTTP/REST or gRPC/Protocol Buffers. This platform is platform and language-neutral as you may make an HTTP call using any programming language.

TensorFlow Lite

TensorFlow Lite is a lightweight deep learning framework to deploy models to mobile devices (iOS and Android) or embedded devices (Raspberry Pi or Edge TPUs). Developers may pick a trained model, convert the model into a compressed fat buffer, and deploy to a mobile or embedded device with TensorFlow Lite.

TensorFlow.js

TensorFlow.js enables developers to deploy their models to web browsers or Node.js environments. Developers can also build and train models in JavaScript in the browser using a Keras-like API.

With TensorFlow 2.0, the capability and parity across platforms and components are greatly improved with standardized exchange formats and aligning APIs. The new simplified architecture of TensorFlow 2.0 is shown by the TensorFlow team in Figure 1-2.

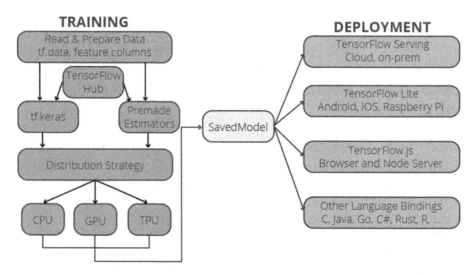

Figure 1-2. *A Simplified Diagram for the TensorFlow 2.0 Architecture*[3]

Improved Experimentation Experience for Researchers

Researchers often need an easy-to-use tool to take their research ideas from concept to code. A proof of concept may only be achieved after several iterations and the concept may be published after several

[3]WHAT'S COMING IN TENSORFLOW 2.0 - TENSORFLOW - MEDIUM, https://medium.com/tensorflow/whats-coming-in-tensorflow-2-0-d3663832e9b8 (last visited Jun 8, 2020)

experiments. TensorFlow 2.0 aims to make it easier to achieve this process. Keras Functional API – paired with Model Subclassing API – offers enough capability to build complex models. `tf.GradientTape` and `tf.custom_gradient` are essential to generate a custom training logic.

Any machine learning project starts with a proof of concept (POC). Developers need to adopt an agile methodology and use easy-to-use tools to take new ideas from concept to evidence-backed publication. Finally, TensorFlow 2.0 offers powerful extensions such as Ragged Tensors, TensorFlow Probability, and Tensor2Tensor to ensure flexibility and increased experimentation capability.

TensorFlow Competitors

Even though this book uses TensorFlow as the primary deep learning framework, it is essential to provide a brief introduction to competing deep learning frameworks and libraries. Although the total number of deep learning frameworks is more than 20, many of them are not currently maintained by their designers. Therefore, we can only talk about a handful of active and reliable deep learning frameworks, which are covered as follows.

Keras

K   Keras is an open source neural network library written in Python which can run on top of TensorFlow, Microsoft Cognitive Toolkit (CNTK), Theano, R, and PlaidML. François Chollet, *a Google engineer*, designed Keras to enable fast experimentation with neural networks. It is very user-friendly, modular, and extensible. Keras also takes pride in being simple, flexible, and powerful. Due to these features, Keras is viewed as the go-to deep learning library by newcomers.

Keras should be regarded as a complementary option to TensorFlow rather than a rival library since it relies on the existing deep learning frameworks. In 2017, Google's TensorFlow team agreed to support Keras in its core library. With TensorFlow 2.0, the Keras API has become more streamlined and integrated. This book takes advantage of TensorFlow Keras API, which makes it much easier to create neural networks.

Keras Official Website: `www.keras.io`

PyTorch

⟳ PyTorch PyTorch is an open source neural network library primarily developed and maintained by Facebook's AI Research Lab (FAIR) and initially released in October 2016. FAIR built PyTorch on top of Torch library, another open source machine learning library, a scientific computing framework, and a scripting language based on the Lua programming language, initially designed by Ronan Collobert, Samy Bengio, and Johnny Mariéthoz.

Since PyTorch is developed by Facebook and offers an easy-to-use interface, its popularity has gained momentum in recent years, particularly in academia. PyTorch is the main competitor of TensorFlow. Prior to TensorFlow 2.0, despite the issues on the ease of use of its APIs, TensorFlow has kept its popularity due to its community support, production performance, and additional use-case solutions. Besides, the latest improvements with TensorFlow 2.0 have introduced remedies to the shortcomings of TensorFlow 1.x. Therefore, TensorFlow will most likely keep its place despite the rising popularity of PyTorch.

PyTorch Official Website: `www.pytorch.org`

Apache MXNet

mxnet MXNet is an open source deep learning framework introduced by Apache Foundation. It is a flexible, scalable, and fast deep learning framework. It has support in multiple programming languages (including C++, Python, Java, Julia, MATLAB, JavaScript, Go, R, Scala, Perl, and Wolfram Language).

MXNet is used and supported by Amazon, Intel, Baidu, Microsoft, Wolfram Research, Carnegie Mellon, MIT, and the University of Washington. Although several respected institutions and tech companies support MXNet, the community support of MXNet is limited. Therefore, it remains less popular compared to TensorFlow, Keras, and PyTorch.

MXNet Official Website: `mxnet.apache.org`

CNTK (Microsoft Cognitive Toolkit)

Microsoft
Cognitive
Toolkit Microsoft released CNTK as its open source deep learning framework in January 2016. CNTK, also called the Microsoft Cognitive Toolkit, has support in popular programming languages such as Python, C++, C#, and Java. Microsoft utilized the use of CNTK in its popular application and products such as Skype, Xbox, and Cortana, particularly for voice, handwriting, and image recognition. However, as of January 2019, Microsoft stopped releasing new updates to the Microsoft Cognitive Toolkit. Therefore, CNTK is considered deprecated.

Microsoft Cognitive Toolkit Official Website: `www.cntk.ai`

Final Evaluation

The designers and the maintainers of the abovementioned deep learning frameworks evidently show a shift in the deep learning framework development. Deep learning started as an academic research field in the universities with little to no real-life applications. However, this has changed with the increasing computing power with lower processing costs and with the rise of the Internet. An increasing number of real-life use cases of deep learning applications have been feeding the appetites of the large tech companies. The earlier academic projects such as Torch, Caffe, and Theano have paved the way for the development of deep learning libraries such as TensorFlow, Keras, and PyTorch. The industry players such as Google, Amazon, and Facebook have hired the maintainers of these earlier projects for their own open source deep learning frameworks. Therefore, the support for the earlier projects is nonexistent to very limited, while the new generation frameworks are becoming increasingly more powerful.

As of 2020, it is safe to state that the real competition is taking place between TensorFlow and PyTorch. Due to its maturity, extensive support in multiple programming languages, popularity in the job market, extensive community support, and supporting technologies, TensorFlow has the upper hand. In 2018, Jeff Hale developed a power ranking for the deep learning frameworks in the market. He weighs the mentions found in the online job listings, the relevant articles and the blog posts, and on GitHub. His results also support the preceding evaluation; see Figure 1-3.

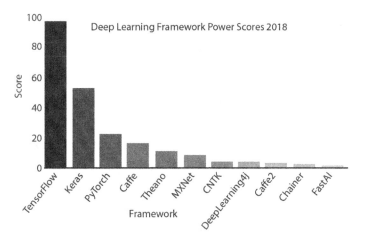

Figure 1-3. *Deep Learning Framework Power Scores 2018 by Jeff Hale[4]*

Therefore, due to its technological advancement and its popularity in the tech community, TensorFlow is the single deep learning framework used in this book. In the next section, we take a look at the new features introduced with TensorFlow 2.0.

Final Considerations

The rising popularity of rival libraries offering easy-to-use modules such as PyTorch was an indication that TensorFlow 1.x was not on the right track. The rise of Keras library with its sole purpose to facilitate the use of TensorFlow – along with a few others – was another indication that TensorFlow must streamline its workflow to keep its existing user base. TensorFlow 2.0 was introduced to mitigate this problem, and it seems that most of the criticism was addressed with both newly introduced APIs and improved existing APIs.

---

[4]Deep Learning Framework Power Scores 2018 Towards Data Science, https://towardsdatascience.com/deep-learning-framework-power-scores-2018-23607ddf297a (last visited Jun 6, 2020)

Installation and Environment Setup

Since we addressed the question of why TensorFlow is the selected deep learning framework for this book and why Python is the selected programming language, it is time to set up a programming environment for deep learning.

Machine learning tasks require continuous testing and proof of concept work. Traditional Python running environments may hinder the speed of testing. Therefore, developers usually resort to interactive running environments for data cleaning, model building, and training. There are several advantages to using interactive environments:

- With interactive running environments, developers can run the part of code, and the outputs are still kept in the memory.

- The next part of the code may still use the output from the previous part of the code.

- Errors given in one part of the code may be fixed, and the rest of the code may still be run.

- A large code file may be broken into pieces, which makes debugging extremely simple.

We can pretty much say that using an interactive programming environment has become an industry standard for deep learning studies. Therefore, we will also follow this practice for the deep learning projects throughout this book.

There are several viable options to build and train models on interactive programming environments for Python TensorFlow programmers. However, we will dive into the most popular options which offer different benefits for their users: (i) **Jupyter Notebook** and (ii) **Google Colab**.

Interactive Programming Environments: IPython, Jupyter Notebook, and Google Colab

There are several tools used in Python interactive programming environments. The central technology making interaction possible is IPython. IPython is an improved shell and read–eval–print loop (REPL) for Python. "IPython Notebook" is a product developed with IPython accessed as a "notebook" via a web browser. IPython handles two fundamental roles:

- The Terminal IPython as a REPL

- The IPython kernel that provides computation and communication with the front-end interfaces such as IPython Notebook

Developers can write codes, take notes, and upload media to their IPython Notebook. The growth of the IPython Notebook project led to the creation of Project Jupyter, which contains the notebook tool and the other interactive tools for multiple languages (Julia, Python, and R). Jupyter Notebook and its flexible interface extend the notebook beyond code to visualization, multimedia, collaboration, and many other features, which creates a comfortable environment for data scientists and machine learning experts.

If you want your development experience to the next step, Google Cloud, which is a cloud-based Jupyter Notebook environment, is the ultimate tool. Google Colab, additionally, offers collaboration options, access to Google's computing power, and cloud-based hosting features. The relationship between IPython, Jupyter Notebook, and Google Colab is shown in Figure 1-4.

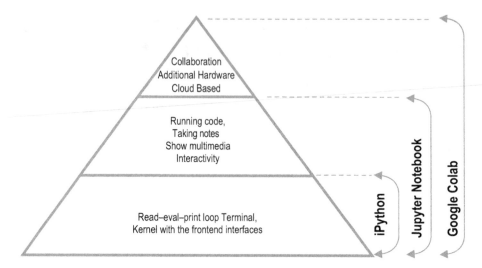

Figure 1-4. *The Relation Between IPython, Jupyter Notebook, and Google Colab*

In the next sections, we dive into the details of IPython, Jupyter Notebook, and Google Colab. We will also (i) install Jupyter Notebook with Anaconda distribution and (ii) setup Google Colab.

IPython

IPython is a command shell and a kernel, which powers interactive Python notebooks. IPython allows programmers to run their code in a notebook environment quickly. IPython provides several features:

- Interactive shells (Terminal and Qt Console)

- A web-based notebook interface with support for code, text, and media

- Support for interactive data visualization and GUI toolkits

- Flexible and embeddable interpreters to load into projects

- Parallel computing toolkits

IPython Project has grown beyond running Python scripts and is on its way to becoming a language-agnostic tool. As of IPython 4.0, the language-agnostic parts are gathered under a new project, named Project Jupyter. The name Jupyter is a reference to core programming languages supported by Jupyter, which are Julia, Python, and R. As of the implementation of this spin-off decision, IPython, now, only focuses on interactive Python, and Jupyter focuses on tools like the notebook format, message protocol, QT Console, and notebook web application.

Jupyter Notebook

jupyter

Project Jupyter is a spin-off open source project born out of IPython Project in 2014. Jupyter is forever free for all to use, and it is developed through the consensus of the Jupyter community. There are several useful tools released as part of Jupyter Project, such as Jupyter Notebook, JupyterLab, Jupyter Hub, and Voilà. While all these tools may be used simultaneously for accompanying purposes, installing Jupyter Notebook suffices the environment requirements of this book.

On the other hand, as an open source project, Jupyter tools may be integrated into different toolsets and bundles. Instead of going through installing Jupyter Notebook through Terminal (for macOS and Linux) or Command Prompt (for Windows), we will use Anaconda distribution, which will make the environment installation on local machines.

Anaconda Distribution

○
ANACONDA "Anaconda is a free and open source distribution of the Python and R programming languages for scientific computing, that aims to simplify package management and deployment."

Environment setup is one of the cumbersome tasks for programming. Developers often encounter unique problems, mainly due to their operating system and its version. With Anaconda distribution, one can easily install Jupyter Notebook and other useful data science libraries.

Installing on Windows

1. Download Anaconda Installer at `www.anaconda.com/products/individual` by selecting the 64-Bit Graphical Installer for Python 3.x; see Figure 1-5.

Anaconda Installers

Windows ■	MacOS ■	Linux △
Python 3.8	Python 3.8	Python 3.8
64-Bit Graphical Installer (466 MB)	64-Bit Graphical Installer (462 MB)	64-Bit (x86) Installer (550 MB)
32-Bit Graphical Installer (397 MB)	64-Bit Command Line Installer (454 MB)	64-Bit (Power8 and Power9) Installer (290 MB)

Figure 1-5. *Anaconda Installer Page*

2. Double-click the installer to launch.

3. Click the "Next" button.

4. Read the licensing agreement, and click "I agree."

5. Select an install for "Just Me," and click the "Next" button.

6. Select a destination folder to install Anaconda and click the "Next" button (make sure that your destination path does not contain spaces or Unicode characters).

7. Make sure (i) "Add Anaconda3 to your PATH environment variable" option is unchecked and (ii) "Register Anaconda3 as my default Python 3.x" option is checked, as shown in Figure 1-6.

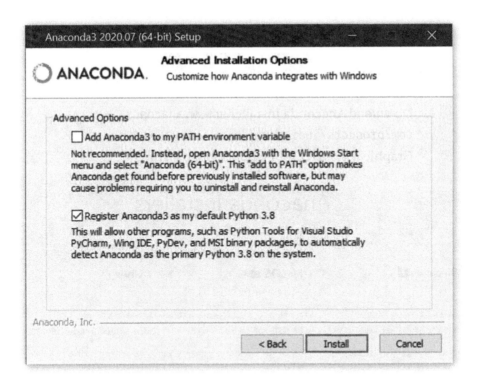

Figure 1-6. *Anaconda Installation Window for Windows OS*

8. Click the "Install" button, and wait for the installation to complete.

9. Click the "Next" button.

10. Click the "Next" button to skip installing PyCharm IDE.

11. After a successful installation, you will see the "Thank you for installing Anaconda Individual Edition" message. Click the "Finish" button.

12. You can now open Jupyter Notebook by finding the "Anaconda-Navigator" app on your Start menu. Just open the app, and click the "Launch" button in the Jupyter Notebook card. This step will prompt a web browser on localhost:8888.

Installing on Mac

1. Download Anaconda Installer at www.anaconda.com/products/individual by selecting the 64-Bit Graphical Installer for Python 3.x; see Figure 1-7.

Anaconda Installers

Windows ⊞	MacOS	Linux △
Python 3.8	Python 3.8	Python 3.8
64-Bit Graphical Installer (466 MB)	64-Bit Graphical Installer (462 MB)	64-Bit (x86) Installer (550 MB)
32-Bit Graphical Installer (397 MB)	64-Bit Command Line Installer (454 MB)	64-Bit (Power8 and Power9) Installer (290 MB)

Figure 1-7. *Anaconda Installer Page*

2. Double-click the downloaded file, and click the "Continue" button to start the installation.

3. Click the "Continue" buttons on the Introduction, Read Me, and License screens.

4. Click the "Agree" button on the prompt window to agree to the terms of the software license agreement.

5. Make sure "Install for me only" option is selected in the Destination Select screen, and click the "Continue" button.

6. Click the Install button to install Anaconda, and wait until the installation is completed.

7. Click the "Continue" button to skip installing the PyCharm IDE.

8. Click the "Close" button, as shown in Figure 1-8, to close the installer.

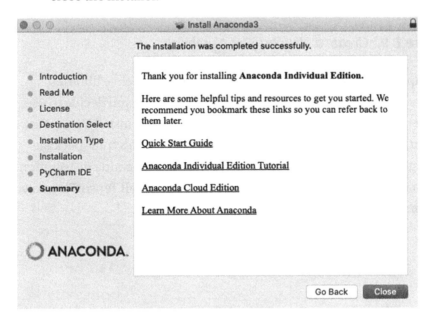

Figure 1-8. *Anaconda Installation Window for macOS*

9. You can now open Jupyter Notebook by finding the "Anaconda-Navigator" app under your Launchpad. Just open the app and click the "Launch" button in the Jupyter Notebook card. This step will prompt a Terminal and a web browser on localhost:8888.

10. You can create a new IPython Notebook by clicking New ➤ Python3, as shown in Figure 1-9.

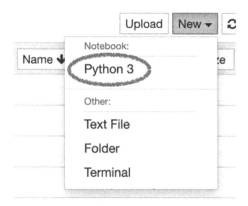

Figure 1-9. *Create a New Jupyter Notebook*

Jupyter Notebook comes with important data science libraries such as Pandas, NumPy, and Matplotlib. However, if you decide to use Jupyter Notebook for deep learning, you still have to install TensorFlow. TensorFlow installation can be achieved with Python's "pip" package manager since we already installed Python with Anaconda distribution. You may follow one of the following methods to install TensorFlow to your local machine.

Operating System	Alternative Methods to Install TensorFlow
macOS	For Mac, just open a Terminal window from Launchpad under Other folder and paste the following script: `pip install --upgrade tensorflow`
Windows	For Windows, go to the "Start" menu on your Windows machine, search for "cmd," right-click it and choose "Run as administrator," and paste the same script mentioned earlier: `pip install --upgrade tensorflow`
macOS/ Windows	For both macOS and Windows, create a new IPython Notebook, as shown earlier. Copy and paste the following code to an empty cell and click the "Run" button, located on the top of the page: `!pip install --upgrade tensorflow`

Note   Beware of the exclamation point!

On the other hand, if you would like to use Google Colab, you don't have to install TensorFlow since Google Colab Notebooks come with preinstalled TensorFlow.

Google Colab

Colaboratory, or Colab for short, is a Google product, which allows developers to write and execute Python code through a browser. Google Colab is an excellent tool for deep learning tasks. Google Colab is a hosted Jupyter Notebook that requires no setup and has an excellent free version, which gives free access to Google computing resources such as GPUs.

As in Anaconda distribution, Google Colab comes with important data science libraries such as Pandas, NumPy, Matplotlib, and – more importantly – TensorFlow. Colab also allows sharing the notebooks with other developers and saves your file to Google Drive. You can access and run your code in the Colab Notebook from anywhere.

In summary, Colab is just a specialized version of the Jupyter Notebook, which runs on the cloud and offers free computing resources.

Caution   As a reader, you may opt to use a local device and install Anaconda distribution shown earlier. Using Jupyter Notebook will not cause any problem as long as you are familiar with Jupyter Notebook. On the other hand, to be able to keep this book and the code up to date, I will deliberately use Google Colab so that I can revisit the code and make updates. Therefore, you will always have access to the latest version of the code. Therefore, **I recommend you to use Google Colab for this book.**

Google Colab Setup

The Google Setup process is relatively easy and can be completed with the following steps across all devices:

1. Visit colab.research.google.com, which will direct you to the Google Colaboratory Welcome Page; see Figure 1-10.

2. Click the "Sign in" button on the right top.

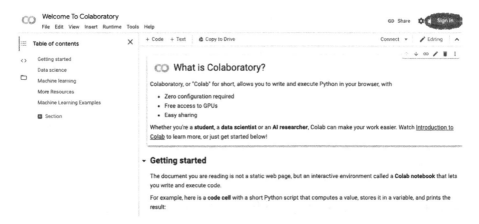

Figure 1-10. *A Screenshot of Google Colab Welcome Notebook*

3. Sign in with your Gmail account. Create one if you don't have a Gmail account; see Figure 1-11.

Figure 1-11. *Google Sign in Page*

4. As soon as you complete the sign-in process, you are ready to use Google Colab.

5. You may easily create a new Colab Notebook on this page by clicking File ➤ New notebook. You can see an example Colab notebook in Figure 1-12.

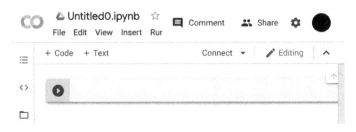

Figure 1-12. *A Screenshot of Empty Google Colab Notebook*

Hardware Options and Requirements

Deep learning is computationally very intensive, and large deep learning projects require multiple machines working simultaneously with distributed computing. Processing units such as CPUs, GPUs, and TPUs, RAM, hard drives such as HDD and SSD, and, finally, power supply units are important hardware units affecting the overall training performance of a computer.

For projects using enormous datasets for training, having an abundant computing power along with the right set of hardware is extremely crucial. The most critical component for model training with large datasets is the processing unit. Developers often use GPUs and TPUs when the task is too big, whereas CPUs may be sufficient for small to medium-size training tasks.

This book does not contain computationally hungry projects since such projects may discourage and demotivate the reader. Therefore, the average computer suffices the computational power requirements for this book. Besides, if you follow the tutorials with Google Colab, as recommended, the sources offered in Google Colab – which include GPUs, as well – are more than enough for the projects in this book. Therefore, you do not have to worry about your hardware at all.

## CHAPTER 2

Introduction to Machine Learning

This chapter aims to make an introduction to the field of machine learning and to clarify the scope of similar domains, particularly deep learning. It also aims to compare different machine learning approaches, introduce some of the popular machine learning models, mention significant machine learning concepts, and walk you through the steps of machine learning. This chapter is a very significant one since deep learning is a subsection of machine learning, and therefore, most explanations are also valid for deep learning.

What Is Machine Learning?

As we all know, computers do not have cognitive abilities, and they cannot reason on their own. However, they are perfect at processing data, and they can complete difficult calculation tasks in a small amount of time. They can process anything so long as we provide them with detailed, step-by-step logical and mathematical instructions. So, if we can represent the cognitive abilities of a human with logical operations, computers can develop cognitive skills.

© Orhan Gazi Yalçın 2021
O. G. Yalçın, *Applied Neural Networks with TensorFlow 2*,
https://doi.org/10.1007/978-1-4842-6513-0_2

Consciousness is one of the hotly debated topics in artificial intelligence: *Can computers become conscious?* While the scope of this discussion is on if machines can mimic human consciousness altogether (*general AI*), in this book, we focus on mimicking particular human skills for specific tasks (*narrow AI*). That's where machine learning comes in.

The term "machine learning" was first coined in 1959 by Arthur Samuel, an IBM scientist and pioneer in the field of computer gaming and artificial intelligence. Throughout the 1950s, 1960s, and 1970s, the early work on the neural networks was conducted with the goal to mimic human brain. However, real-life applications of neural networks were unfeasible for a long time due to the limitations of computer technology. The fundamental machine learning research on other ML techniques (i.e., non-deep learning techniques which require fewer computer resources) was popularized in the 1980s and 1990s. The advancements in computer technology during this period partially allowed the adoption of machine learning applications in real life. As the years passed, the limitations due to immature computer technology were mostly eliminated, particularly, in recent years. Although we always strive for better and more efficient computing power and storage, now, we can at least quickly build models, test them, and even deploy on the Internet for the whole world to use. Today, the field of machine learning is very vibrant thanks to the abundance of data, efficient data storage technologies, and faster and cheaper processing power. Figure 2-1 summarizes timeline of artificial intelligence.

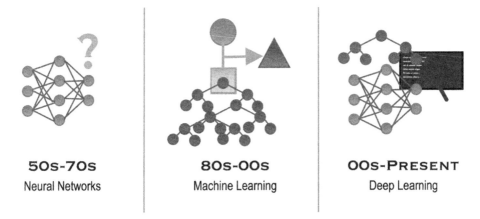

5Os-7Os	8Os-OOs	OOs-Present
Neural Networks	Machine Learning	Deep Learning

Figure 2-1. *Timeline of Artificial Intelligence*

Machine learning is considered as a sub-discipline under the field of artificial intelligence. Machine learning (ML) studies aim to automatically improve the performance of the computer algorithms designed for particular tasks with experience. In a machine learning study, the experience is derived from the training data, which may be defined as the sample data collected on previously recorded observations. Through this experience, machine learning algorithms can learn and build mathematical models to make predictions and decisions. The learning process starts with feeding training data (e.g., examples, direct experience, basic instructions), which contains implicit patterns, into the model. Since computers have more processing power than humans, they can find these valuable patterns in the data within a short amount of time. These patterns are – then – used to make predictions and decisions on relevant events. The learning may continue even after deployment if the developer builds a suitable machine learning system which allows continuous training.

> *Previously, we might use machine learning in a few sub-components of a system. Now we actually use machine learning to replace entire sets of systems, rather than trying to make a better machine learning model for each of the pieces.*
>
> —Jeff Dean

There is an ever-increasing use of machine learning applications in different fields. These real-life applications vary to a great extent. Some use cases may be listed as follows:

- **Healthcare:** Medical diagnosis given the patient's symptoms

- **Ecommerce**: Predicting the expected demand

- **Law**: Reviewing legal documents and alerting lawyers about problematic provisions

- **Social Network**: Finding a good match given the user's preferences on a dating app

- **Finance**: Predicting the future price of a stock given the historical data

This is obviously a non-exhaustive list, and there are hundreds, if not thousands, of potential machine learning use cases. Depending on what your goal is, there are many different methods to create a machine learning model. These methods are usually grouped under four main approaches: (i) supervised learning, (ii) semi-supervised learning, (iii) unsupervised learning, and (iv) reinforcement learning.

Each method contains distinct differences in their design, but they all follow the same underlying principles and conform to the same theoretical background. In the upcoming sections, we will cover these different approaches in more detail. But first, we will briefly talk about the scope of adjacent fields: (i) artificial intelligence, (ii) deep learning, (iii) big data, and (iv) data science.

Scope of Machine Learning and Its Relation to Adjacent Fields

Once you start consuming machine learning contents such as books, articles, video courses, and blog posts, you will often see terms such as artificial intelligence, machine learning, deep learning, big data, and data science. There is a slight level of ambiguity about the differences between these terms. In this section, we clarify this ambiguity and state the differences.

Artificial Intelligence

Artificial intelligence (AI) is a broad umbrella term, and its definition varies across different textbooks. The term AI is often used to describe computers that simulate human intelligence and mimic "cognitive" abilities that humans associate with the human mind. Problem-solving and learning are examples of these cognitive abilities. The field of AI contains machine learning studies since AI systems are capable of learning from experiences. Generally speaking, machines with artificial intelligence are capable of

- Understanding and interpreting data

- Learning from data

- Making "intelligent" decisions based on insights and patterns extracted from data

These terms are highly associated with machine learning. Thanks to machine learning, AI systems can learn and excel at their level of consciousness. Machine learning is used to train AI systems and make them smarter.

Deep Learning

Deep learning (DL) is a subfield of machine learning that exclusively uses multiple layers of neurons to extract patterns and features from raw data. These multiple layers of interconnected neurons create artificial neural networks (ANNs); see Figure 2-2. An ANN is a special machine learning algorithm designed to simulate the working mechanism of the human brain. There are many different types of artificial neural networks intended for several purposes. In summary, deep learning algorithms are a subset of machine learning algorithms.

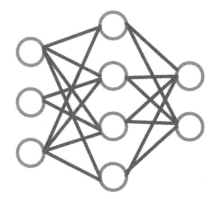

Figure 2-2. *An Artificial Neural Network*

Just as in machine learning, all four approaches (supervised, semi-supervised, unsupervised, and reinforcement learning) can be utilized in deep learning. When there is an abundance of data and enough computing power, deep learning almost always outperforms the other machine learning algorithms. Deep learning algorithms are especially useful in image processing, voice recognition, and machine translation.

Data Science

Data science is an interdisciplinary field that sits at the intersection of artificial intelligence, particular domain knowledge, information science, and statistics. Data scientists use various scientific methods, processes, and algorithms to obtain knowledge and draw insights from observed data.

In contrast with machine learning, the goal of a data science study does not have to be model training. Data science studies often aim to extract knowledge and insight to support the human decision-making process without creating an AI system. Therefore, although there is an intersection between data science and the other adjacent fields, the field of data science differs from them since it does not have to deliver an intelligent system or a trained model.

Big Data

Big data is a field that aims to efficiently analyze a large amount of data that cannot be processed with traditional data processing methods and applications. Data with more observation usually brings more accuracy, while high complexity may increase false discovery rates. The field of big data studies on how to efficiently capture, store, analyze, search, share, visualize, and update data when the size of a dataset is very large. Big data studies can be used both in artificial intelligence (and its subfields) and in data science. Big data sits at the intersection of all the other fields mentioned earlier since its methods are crucial for all of them.

The Taxonomy Diagram

The relationship between these adjacent terms may be visualized in the following taxonomy diagram, as shown in Figure 2-3.

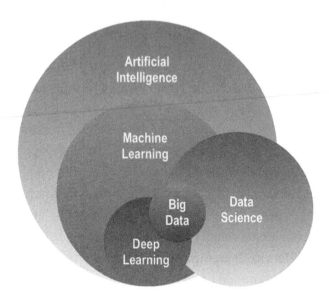

Figure 2-3. *The Taxonomy of Artificial Intelligence and Data Science*

This taxonomy is almost a clear evidence for the reasons behind the ambiguity. Whenever we are talking about deep learning, we are also talking about machine learning and artificial intelligence. When we are working on a deep learning project, some might call it a data science project or a big data project. These naming practices are not necessarily incorrect, but they are confusing. Therefore, it is vital to know the intersections and subtractions of these fields.

Machine Learning Approaches and Models

Top machine learning approaches are categorized depending on the nature of their feedback mechanism for learning. These different approaches may be listed as follows:

- Supervised learning

- Unsupervised learning

- Semi-supervised learning

- Reinforcement learning

Most of the machine learning problems may be addressed by adopting one of these approaches. Yet, we may still encounter complex machine learning solutions that do not fit into one of these approaches. In this section, we will briefly cover the scope of these four main machine learning approaches, along with their application examples. This taxonomy is crucial in the sense that it will help you to quickly uncover the nature of a problem you may encounter in the future, analyze your resources, and develop a suitable solution. Let's start with the supervised learning approach.

Supervised Learning

The supervised learning approach can be adopted when there is a dataset containing the records of the response variable values (or labels). Depending on the context, this data with labels is usually referred to as "labeled data" and "training data." For example, when we try to predict a person's height using their weight, age, and gender, we need the training data that contains people's weight, age, and gender info along with their real heights. This data allows the machine learning algorithm to discover the relationship between height and the other variables. Then, using this knowledge, the model can predict the height of a given person.

For example, we can mark emails as "spam" or "not spam" based on the differentiating features of the previously seen spam and not-spam emails such as the lengths of the emails and use of particular keywords in the emails. Learning from training data continues until the machine learning model achieves a high level of accuracy on the training data.

There are two main supervised learning problems: (i) classification problems and (ii) regression problems. In classification problems, the models learn to classify an observation based on their variable values.

During the learning process, the model is exposed to a lot of observations with their labels. For example, after seeing thousands of customers with their shopping habits and gender information, a model may successfully predict the gender of a new customer based on their shopping habits. Binary classification is the term used for grouping under two labels such as male and female. Another binary classification example might be predicting whether the animal in a picture is a "cat" or "not cat," as shown in Figure 2-4.

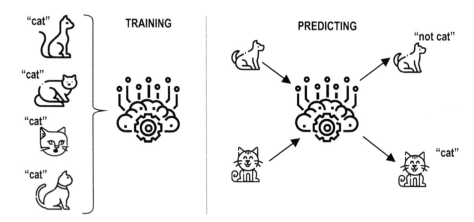

Figure 2-4. *Classification Problem in Supervised Learning*[1]

On the other hand, multilabel classification is used when there are more than two labels. Identifying and predicting handwritten letters and number on an image would be an example of multilabel classification.

In regression problems, the goal is to calculate a value by taking advantage of the relationship between the other variables (*i.e., independent variables, explanatory variables, or features*) and the target variable (*i.e., dependent variable, response variable, or label*). The strength of the relationship between our target variable and the other variables

---

[1]Icons made by Freepik, Those icons, Eucalyp from www.flaticon.com

is a critical determinant of the prediction value, along with the values of the explanatory variables for the observation. Predicting how much a customer would spend based on its historical data is a regression problem.

There are dozens of different machine learning algorithms suitable for supervised learning. Since the focus of this book is on deep learning, we only cover some of the more popular ones without going into their details.

- **Linear and Logistic Regression**: Linear regression is a linear approach to model the relationship between a numerical response variable (Y) and one or more explanatory variables (Xs). Logistic regression, on the other hand, is a slightly different method to model the probability of a particular class or event to exist, such as male/female for gender. Therefore, linear regression is used for regression problems, whereas logistic regression is *mostly* used for classification problems.

- **Decision Trees and Ensemble Methods**: A decision tree is a flowchart-like structure and a decision support tool that connects the potential decisions and uncertain events with their probabilities to create a model that predicts possible outcomes. We can also ensemble multiple decision trees to create more advanced machine learning algorithms such as **random forest** algorithm.

- **Support Vector Machines**: A support vector machine constructs a hyperplane to separate a space which can be used for classification, regression, or outlier detection. For example, a three-dimensional space (*e.g., a cube*) can be separated into smaller pieces with a two-dimensional hyperplane (*e.g., a square*). This will help to group observations into two different classes. The potential applications can be much more complicated than this example. Support vector machine is a popular machine learning algorithm due to its high accuracy performance and relatively low-level computing source requirements.

- **K-Nearest Neighbors**: The k-nearest neighbors algorithm is a machine learning algorithm that may be used for classification and regression problems. k is a user-defined constant, which represents the number of neighbor observations to be included in the algorithm. In classification problems, the neighbors of a new unlabeled observation are used to predict the label of this new observation based on the labels of the neighbors.

- **Neural Networks (Multilayer Perceptron, MLP)**: Feedforward only neural networks, convolutional neural networks (CNNs), and recurrent neural networks (RNNs) are often used in supervised learning problems, which will be covered in the upcoming chapters.

Unsupervised Learning

Unsupervised learning is an approach used in machine learning algorithms to draw inferences from the datasets which do not contain labels. Unsupervised learning is mainly used in clustering analysis. Clustering analysis is a grouping effort in which the members of a group (i.e., a cluster) are more similar to each other than the members of the other clusters. There are many different clustering methods available. They usually utilize a type of similarity measure based on selected metrics such as Euclidean or probabilistic distance. Bioinformatic sequence analysis, genetic clustering, pattern mining, and object recognition are some of the clustering problems which may be tackled with the unsupervised learning approach.

Another use case of unsupervised learning is dimensionality reduction. Dimensionality is equivalent to the number of features used in a dataset. In some datasets, you may find hundreds of potential features stored in individual columns. In most of these datasets, several of these columns are highly correlated. Therefore, we should either select the best ones, *feature selection*, or extract new features combining the existing ones, *feature extraction*. This is where unsupervised learning comes into play. Dimensionality reduction methods help us create neater and cleaner models that are free of noise and unnecessary features.

Unsupervised learning may also be used in anomaly detection problems and generative systems. I will briefly mention some of the popular unsupervised machine learning models as follows:

- **Hierarchical Clustering**: Hierarchical clustering is an unsupervised machine learning algorithm used to group the unlabeled observations having similar characteristics incrementally. Hierarchical clustering can be agglomerative (bottom-up approach) or divisive (top-down approach). The hierarchy of the clusters is represented as a tree or a dendrogram.

- **K-Means Clustering**: K-means clustering is a popular unsupervised machine learning algorithm. K is a user-assigned constant representing the number of clusters to be created. K-means clustering groups observations into k distinct clusters based on the distance to the center of a cluster.

- **Principal Component Analysis (PCA)**: PCA is widely used for dimensionality reduction. PCA finds a linear combination of two or more variables, which are called principal components. This procedure reduces the dimensional complexity of the model so that the problem may be visualized and analyzed more quickly as the model is trained more easily as well.

- **Neural Networks**: Autoencoders, deep belief nets, Hebbian learning, generative adversarial networks (GANs), and self-organizing maps are some of the neural networks used for unsupervised learning. The details and the applications of some of these network structures will be covered in the upcoming chapters.

Semi-supervised Learning

Semi-supervised learning is a machine learning approach that combines the characteristics of supervised learning and unsupervised learning. A semi-supervised learning approach is particularly useful when we have a small amount of labeled data with a large amount of unlabeled data available for training. Supervised learning characteristics help take advantage of the small amount of label data. In contrast, unsupervised learning characteristics are useful to take advantage of a large amount of unlabeled data.

Well, you might think that if there are useful real-life applications for semi-supervised learning. Although supervised learning is a powerful approach, labeling data – to be used in supervised learning – is a costly and time-consuming process. On the other hand, a large amount of data can also be beneficial even though they are not labeled. So, in real life, the semi-supervised learning may shine out as the most suitable and the most fruitful machine learning approach if done correctly.

In semi-supervised learning, we usually start by clustering the unlabeled data. Then, we use the labeled data to label the clustered unlabeled data. Finally, a significant amount of now-labeled data is used to train machine learning models. Semi-supervised learning models can be very powerful since they can take advantage of a high volume of data.

Semi-supervised learning models are usually a combination of transformed and adjusted versions of the existing machine learning algorithms used in supervised and unsupervised learning. This approach is successfully used in areas like speech analysis, content classification, and protein sequence classification. The similarity of these fields is that they offer abundant unlabeled data and only a small amount of labeled data.

Reinforcement Learning

Reinforcement learning is one of the primary approaches to machine learning concerned with finding optimal agent actions that maximize the reward within a particular environment. The agent learns to perfect its actions to gain the highest possible cumulative reward. There are four main elements in reinforcement learning:

- **Agent**: The trainable program which exercises the tasks assigned to it

- **Environment**: The real or virtual universe where the agent completes its tasks

- **Action**: A move of the agent which results in a change of status in the environment

- **Reward**: A negative or positive remuneration based on the action

Reinforcement learning may be used in both the real world and in the virtual world. For instance, you may create an evolving ad placement system deciding how many ads to place to a website based on the ad revenue generated in different setups. The ad placement system would be an excellent example of real-world applications. On the other hand, you can train an agent in a video game with reinforcement learning to compete against other players, which are usually referred to as bots. Finally, virtual and real training of robots in terms of their movements are done with the reinforcement learning approach. Some of the popular reinforcement learning models may be listed as follows:

- Q-Learning

- State-Action-Reward-State-Action (SARSA)

- Deep Q network (DQN)

- Deep Deterministic Policy Gradient (DDPG)

One of the disadvantages of the existing deep learning frameworks is that they lack comprehensive module support for reinforcement learning, and TensorFlow is no exception. Deep reinforcement learning can only be done with extension libraries built on top of existing deep learning libraries such as Keras-RL, TF.Agents, and Tensorforce or dedicated reinforcement learning libraries such as Open AI Baselines and Stable Baselines. Therefore, we will not be able to dive deep into reinforcement learning in this book.

Evaluation of Different Approaches

We briefly covered the four main machine learning approaches: (i) supervised learning, (ii) unsupervised learning, (iii) semi-supervised learning, and (v) reinforcement learning. These approaches are applied to machine learning problems with several potential algorithms. While supervised learning solves classification and regression problems, unsupervised learning deals with dimensionality reduction and clustering. Semi-supervised learning combines supervised learning and unsupervised learning approaches to take advantage of unlabeled data for classification tasks, whereas reinforcement learning is used to find the perfect set of actions for the highest reward. A summary of the characteristics of these approaches may be found in Figure 2-5.

Figure 2-5. *A Summary of the Characteristics of the Machine Learning Approaches*

Steps of Machine Learning

Thanks to the years of machine learning studies, we – now – perfected a machine learning process flow where we can accurately build and train models. Although you might see slightly altered process flows in other sources, the fundamentals remain the same. The steps of a machine learning process may be listed as follows:

- Gathering data
- Preparing data
- Model selection

- Training

- Evaluation

- Hyperparameter tuning

- Prediction

Let's dive into each individual step to see what's happening inside them.

Gathering Data

Data is the fuel of machine learning models. Without proper data, we cannot reach our expected destination: high accuracy. This data must be of high quality as well as in large volumes. Therefore, both the quality and quantity of the gathered data are significant for a successful machine learning project. In fact, gathering data is one of the most challenging parts of machine learning projects. But do not be afraid. Thanks to platforms such as Kaggle and UC Irvine's Repository, we can skip the "gathering data" step, at least for educational purposes. The outcome of this step is a representation of data such as a table saved as a CSV (*comma-separated values*) file.

Preparing Data

Now that we have gathered data, we need to prepare our data for model building and training.

First of all, we make initial cleaning and transformations to our data. This part may include several tasks, including – but not limited to – dealing with missing values, removing duplicates, correcting errors, converting strings to floats, normalizing the data, and generating dummy variables.

Then, we randomize the data to eliminate any unwanted correlation due to the timing of data gathering. After cleaning and randomizing our data, we use data visualization tools to discover relationships between variables that may help us during the model building process. We can also detect class imbalances and outliers with data visualization.

Finally, we split the prepared dataset into training and evaluation (*i.e., test*) datasets.

Model Selection

Depending on our problem, we try different machine learning algorithms to find the best performing model. Without machine learning and deep learning libraries, coding the entire model algorithms would be extremely time-consuming. But thanks to these libraries, we can quickly build our models in several machine learning models and find the best performing one after training with ease.

Training

Now that we have selected an algorithm (or algorithms), built our model (or models), and prepared our data, we can feed this data into the model(s) and watch it (them) optimize the equation variables. The goal of training is to make the highest number of correct predictions or the lowest amount of error. For example, if we are using linear regression, the equation we work on is the following:

$$y = m*x + b$$

Notation:

y: response variable

x: explanatory variable

m: slope

b: intercept

Our linear regression model tries to find the perfect slope (m) and intercept (b) values so that we might end up with the lowest amount of difference in the actual y values and y predictions. The process for perfecting our model is done iteratively over several training steps until no further performance increase on the selected performance metric can be observed.

Evaluation

Immediately after training our model with training data, we should test our trained model with an evaluation dataset that our model has never seen before. This previously unseen data provides us with an objective performance score. The ideal training/test split ratios for datasets are usually 80/20, 90/10, or 70/30, depending on the domain. In some cases, data scientist also set aside a validation dataset.

Especially when we have limited data, one of the useful evaluation techniques used by data scientists is cross-validation. Keep in mind that we will often apply cross-validation for evaluation.

Cross-Validation is an alternative resampling technique used for evaluation. In k-fold cross-validation, the dataset is split into k number of groups. One group is kept as testing data, and this group is switched k times. So, each group is used for testing once. In the end, we have a much more reliable performance evaluation.

Evaluation is a particularly important step to check for overfitting. Machine learning models are overly eager when it comes to optimization. They tend to create a very complex set of variable values to capture all the variance in our data. However, this may lead to problems when we deploy the model in real life since perfecting a model using a limited amount of training data creates a short sighting effect.

Overfitting is a machine learning problem that occurs when the model is too closely fit the observations. When the model has an overfitting problem, it tends to perform well for training data but performs poorly for testing data and in the real world.

Our model should be highly accurate but also flexible. In machine learning studies, we always observe the bias and variance trade-off. There has to be a balance between the level of bias introduced to the system and the level of the variance observed so that our model provides meaningful and reliable predictions in real life.

Bias and Variance Trade-Off is a property of machine learning models. Bias is the assumptions made by the model to simplify the optimization process. Variance is a measure for the spread of the values that a target function can output. While bias brings simplicity to the model, you may be way off to have reliable predictions. On the other hand, a high variance can damage the ability to obtain meaningful results.

These are some of the properties to look out for when evaluating a machine learning model. Let's say we were careful about bias and variance trade-off and overfitting, and we used cross-validation for training our model. But *how are we going to measure the success of our model?* This is where we choose performance terms, depending on our problem.

Performance Terms for Classification We usually refer to the **Confusion matrix** (see Figure 2-6) to understand how our model performed. Confusion matrix does not only allow us to calculate the **accuracy** of the model but also **recall**, **precision**, and **F1-score** of the model performance.

Prediction

		Positive	Negative
Observation	**Positive**	True Positives	False Negatives
	Negative	False Positives	True Negatives

Figure 2-6. *Confusion Matrix for Classification Problems*

Performance Terms for Regression We usually use **error-based metrics** to measure model performance. The difference between real observation and prediction is called an error. With an aggregative calculation, we might find metrics such as **root mean squared error (RMSE), mean absolute error (MSE)**, and other metrics. These metric values are useful to measure the model's success for a particular regression.

Hyperparameter Tuning

Now that we have our performance metric results on both training and test datasets, we can tune our model hyperparameters to increase our performance even further. Learning rate, number of training steps, initialization values, epoch size, batch size, and distribution type are some of the hyperparameters that can be played around with. Hyperparameter tuning is usually referred to as an artwork rather than a science. Data scientists use their intuition to try different combinations of hyperparameters to achieve the highest performance.

Prediction

At this point, we have now completed our initial training with tuned hyperparameters. Now, we can make predictions with our trained model. The prediction step should not be seen as the end of the learning process. After receiving real-world feedbacks, we can go back and train, evaluate, and tune our model further to address the ever-changing nature of the data science problems.

Final Evaluations

In this chapter, we made an introduction to machine learning, which also includes the subfield of deep learning. We compared and contrasted the fields of artificial intelligence, machine learning, deep learning, data science, and big data.

We visited the main machine learning approaches, (i) supervised learning, (ii) unsupervised learning, (iii) semi-supervised learning, and (iv) reinforcement learning, and introduced some of the popular machine learning models used with these approaches.

Then, we covered the steps of machine learning. This section explained the necessary steps to successfully build and train a machine learning model with the data that we gathered and cleaned.

In the next chapter, we will make an introduction to deep learning. The introduction to machine learning will help you to grasp the concepts we will see in the next chapter.

CHAPTER 3

Deep Learning and Neural Networks Overview

Since you are reading this book, it is safe to assume that you know how deep learning has gained popularity in recent years. There is a very good reason for deep learning's increasing popularity: **its uncanny accuracy performance**. Especially when there are abundant data and available processing power, deep learning is the choice of machine learning experts. The performance comparison between deep learning and traditional machine learning algorithms is shown in Figure 3-1.

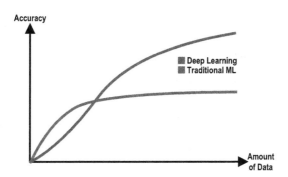

Figure 3-1. *Deep Learning vs. Traditional ML Comparison on Accuracy*

© Orhan Gazi Yalçın 2021
O. G. Yalçın, *Applied Neural Networks with TensorFlow 2,*
https://doi.org/10.1007/978-1-4842-6513-0_3

Deep learning is a subfield of machine learning which imitates data processing and pattern generation capabilities of the human brain for automated decision-making. The distinct accuracy curve of deep learning compared to the other machine learning algorithms contributed to its widespread use and adoption by machine learning experts. Deep learning is made possible thanks to artificial neural networks. Artificial neural network is the network structure that simulates the neurons in human brains so that deep learning can take place. In Figure 3-2, you may find an example of an artificial neural network (ANN) with deep learning capability.

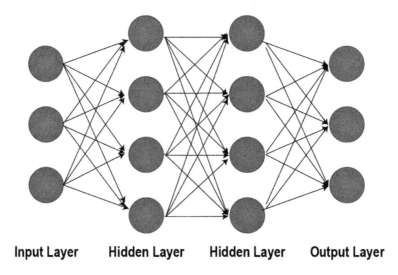

Input Layer   Hidden Layer   Hidden Layer   Output Layer

Figure 3-2. A Depiction of Artificial Neural Networks with Two Hidden Layers

You might think that deep learning is a newly invented field that recently overthrown the other machine learning algorithms. Lots of people think this way. However, the field of artificial neural networks and deep learning dates back to the 1940s. The recent rise of deep learning is mainly due to a high amount of available data and – more importantly – due to cheap and abundant processing power.

This is an overview chapter for deep learning. We will take a look at the critical concepts that we often use in deep learning, including (i) activation functions, (ii) loss functions, (iii) optimizers and backpropagation, (iv) regularization, and (v) feature scaling. But, first, we will dive into the history of artificial neural networks and deep learning so that you will have an idea about the roots of the deep learning concepts which you will often see in this book.

Timeline of Neural Networks and Deep Learning Studies

The timeline of neural networks and deep learning studies does not consist of a series of uninterrupted advancements. In fact, the field of artificial intelligence experienced a few downfalls, which are referred to as AI winters. Let's dive into the history of neural networks and deep learning, which started in 1943.

Development of Artificial Neurons – In 1943, the pioneer academics Walter Pitts and Warren McCulloch published the paper *"A Logical Calculus of the Ideas Immanent in Nervous Activity,"* where they presented a mathematical model of a biological neuron, called **McCulloch-Pitts Neuron**. Capabilities of McCulloch Pitts Neuron are minimal, and it does not have a learning mechanism. The importance of McCulloch Pitts Neuron is that it lays the foundation for deep learning. In 1957, Frank Rosenblatt published another paper, titled "The Perceptron: A Perceiving and Recognizing Automaton," where he introduces the **perceptron** with learning and binary classification capabilities. The revolutionary perceptron model – risen to its place after Mcculloch Pitts Neuron – has inspired many researchers working on artificial neural networks.

Backpropagation – In 1960, Henry J. Kelley published a paper titled "Gradient Theory of Optimal Flight Paths," where he demonstrates an example of continuous backpropagation. Backpropagation is an important deep learning concept that we will cover under this chapter. In 1962, Stuart Dreyfus improved backpropagation with chain rule in his paper, "The Numerical Solution of Variational Problems." The term backpropagation was coined in 1986 by Rumelhart, Hinton, and Williams, and these researchers have popularized its use in artificial neural networks.

Training and Computerization – In 1965, Alexey Ivakhnenko, usually referred to as "Father of Deep Learning," built a hierarchical representation of neural networks and successfully trained this model by using a polynomial activation function. In 1970, Seppo Linnainmaa found automatic differentiation for backpropagation and was able to write the first backpropagation program. This development may be marked as the beginning of the computerization of deep learning. In 1971, Ivakhnenko created an eight-layer neural network, which is considered a deep learning network due to its multilayer structure.

AI Winter – In 1969, Marvin Minsky and Seymour Papert wrote the book Perceptrons in which he fiercely attacks the work of Frank Rosenblatt, the Perceptron. This book caused devastating damage to AI project funds, which triggered **an AI winter** that lasted from 1974 until 1980.

Convolutional Neural Networks – In 1980, Kunihiko Fukushima introduced the neocognitron, the first convolutional neural networks (CNNs), which can recognize visual patterns. In 1982, Paul Werbos proposed the use of backpropagation in neural networks for error minimization, and the AI community has adopted this proposal widely. In 1989, Yann LeCun used backpropagation to train CNNs to recognize handwritten digits in the MNIST (Modified National Institute of Standards and Technology) dataset. In this book, we have a similar case study in Chapter 7.

Recurrent Neural Networks – In 1982, John Hopfield introduced Hopfield network, which is an early implementation of recurrent neural networks (RNNs). Recurrent neural networks are revolutionary algorithms that work best for sequential data. In 1985, Geoffrey Hinton, David H. Ackley, and Terrence Sejnowski proposed Boltzmann Machine, which is a stochastic RNN without an output layer. In 1986, Paul Smolensky developed a new variation of Boltzmann Machine, which does not have intralayer connections in input and hidden layers, which is called a Restricted Boltzmann Machine. Restricted Boltzmann Machines are particularly successful in recommender systems. In 1997, Sepp Hochreiter and Jürgen Schmidhuber published a paper on an improved RNN model, long short-term memory (LSTM), which we will also cover in Chapter 8. In 2006, Geoffrey Hinton, Simon Osindero, and Yee Whye Teh combined several Restricted Boltzmann Machines (RBMs) and created deep belief networks, which improved the capabilities of RBMs.

Capabilities of Deep Learning – In 1986, Terry Sejnowski developed NETtalk, a neural network-based text-to-speech system which can pronounce English text. In 1989, George Cybenko showed in his paper "Approximation by Superpositions of a Sigmoidal Function" that a feedforward neural network with a single hidden layer *can solve any continuous function*.

Vanishing Gradient Problem – In 1991, Sepp Hochreiter discovered and proved the vanishing gradient problem, which slows down the deep learning process and makes it impractical. After 20 years, in 2011, Yoshua Bengio, Antoine Bordes, and Xavier Glorot showed that using Rectified Linear Unit (ReLU) as the activation function can prevent vanishing gradient problem.

GPU for Deep Learning – In 2009, Andrew Ng, Rajat Raina, and Anand Madhavan, with their paper "Large-Scale Deep Unsupervised Learning Using Graphics Processors," recommended the use of GPUs for deep learning since the number of cores found in GPUs is a lot more than the ones in CPUs. This switch reduces the training time of neural networks and makes their applications more feasible. Increasing use of GPUs for deep learning has led to the development of specialized ASICS for deep learning (e.g., Google's TPU) along with official parallel computing platforms introduced by GPU manufacturers (e.g., Nvidia's CUDA and AMD's ROCm).

ImageNet and AlexNet – In 2009, Fei-Fei Li launched a database with 14 million labeled images, called ImageNet. The creation of the ImageNet database has contributed to the development of neural networks for image processing since one of the essential components of deep learning is abundant data. Ever since the creation of the ImageNet database, yearly competitions were held to improve the image processing studies. In 2012, Alex Krizhevsky designed a GPU-trained CNN, AlexNet, which increased the model accuracy by 75% compared to earlier models.

Generative Adversarial Networks – In 2014, Ian Goodfellow came up with the idea of a new neural network model while he was talking with his friends at a local bar. This revolutionary model, which was designed overnight, is now known as generative adversarial neural networks (GANs), which is capable of generating art, text, and poems, and it can complete many other creative tasks. We have a case study for the implementation of GANs in Chapter 12.

Power of Reinforcement Learning – In 2016, DeepMind trained a deep reinforcement learning model, AlphaGo, which can play the game of Go, which is considered a much more complicated game compared to Chess. AlphaGo beat the World Champion Ke Jie in Go in 2017.

Turing Award to the Pioneers of Deep Learning – In 2019, the three pioneers in AI, Yann LeCun, Geoffrey Hinton, and Yoshua Bengio, shared the Turing Award. This award is proof that shows the significance of deep learning for the computer science community.

Structure of Artificial Neural Networks

Before diving into essential deep learning concepts, let's take a look at the journey on the development of today's modern deep neural networks. Today, we can easily find examples of neural networks with hundreds of layers and thousands of neurons, but before the mid twentieth century, the term artificial neural network did not even exist. It all started in 1943 with a simple artificial neuron – McCulloch Pitts Neuron – which can only do simple mathematical calculations with no learning capability.

McCulloch-Pitts Neuron

The McCulloch Pitts Neuron was introduced in 1943, and it is capable of doing only basic mathematical operations. Each event is given a Boolean value (0 or 1), and if the sum of the event outcomes (0s and 1s) surpasses a threshold, then the artificial neuron fires. A visual example for OR and AND operations with McCulloch Pitts Neuron is shown in Figure 3-3.

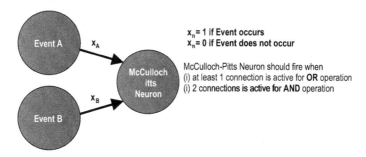

Figure 3-3. *McCulloch Pitts Neuron for OR and AND Operations*

Since the inputs from the events in McCulloch Pitts Neuron can only be Boolean values (0 or 1), its capabilities were minimal. This limitation was addressed with the development of Linear Threshold Unit (LTU).

Linear Threshold Unit (LTU)

In a McCulloch Pitts Neuron, the significance of each event is equal, which is problematic since most real-world events do not conform to this simplistic setting. To address this issue, Linear Threshold Unit (LTU) was introduced in 1957. In an LTU, weights are assigned to each event, and these weights can be negative or positive. The outcome of each even is still given a Boolean value (0 or 1), but then is multiplied with the assigned weight. The LTU is only activated if the sum of these weighted event outcomes is positive. In Figure 3-4, you may find a visualization of LTU, which is the basis for today's artificial neural networks.

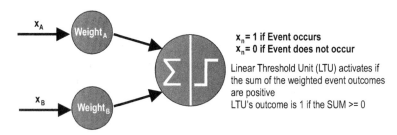

Figure 3-4. Linear Threshold Unit (LTU) Visualization

Perceptron

Perceptron is a binary classification algorithm for supervised learning and consists of a layer of LTUs. In a perceptron, LTUs use the same event outputs as input. The perceptron algorithm can adjust the weights to correct the behavior of the trained neural network. In addition, a bias term may be added to increase the accuracy performance of the network.

When there is only one layer of perceptron, it is called a single-layer perceptron. There is one layer for outputs along with a single input layer that receives the inputs. When hidden layers are added to a single-layer perceptron, we end up with a multilayer perceptron (MLP). An MLP is considered as a type of deep neural network, and the artificial neural networks we build for everyday problems are examples of MLP. In Figure 3-5, you may find an example visualization of single-layer perceptron.

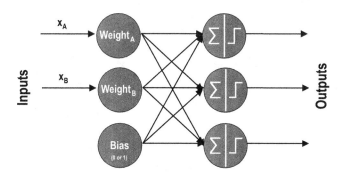

Figure 3-5. *An Example of a Single-Layer Perceptron Diagram*

A Modern Deep Neural Network

The deep neural networks we come across today are improved versions of multilayer perceptrons (MLP). We often use a more complex activation function than a step function (0 or 1) such as ReLU, Sigmoid, Tanh, and Softmax. Modern deep neural networks usually take advantage of one of the gradient descent methods for optimization. An example modern deep neural network is shown in Figure 3-6.

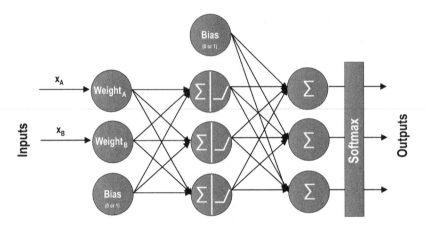

Figure 3-6. *A Modern Deep Neural Network Example*

Now that you know more about the journey to develop today's modern deep neural networks, which started with the McCulloch Pitts Neurons, we can dive into essential deep learning concepts that we use in our applications.

Activation Functions

Activation function is a function used to help artificial neural networks to learn complex patterns from the data. An activation function is usually added to the end of each neuron, which affects what to fire to the next neuron. In other words, as shown in Figure 3-7, the activation function of a neuron gives the output of that neuron after being given an input or set of inputs.

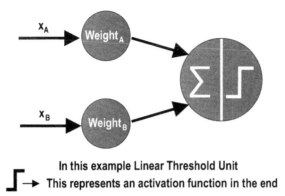

In this example Linear Threshold Unit
→ This represents an activation function in the end

Figure 3-7. *An Example LTU Diagram with Activation Function in the End*

Activation functions introduce a final calculation step that adds additional complexity to artificial neural networks. Therefore, they increase the required training time and processing power. So, why would we use activation functions in neural networks? The answer is simple: Activation functions increase the capabilities of the neural networks to use relevant information and suppress the irrelevant data points. Without activation functions, our neural networks would only be performing a linear transformation. Although avoiding activation functions makes a neural network model simpler, the model will be less powerful and will not be able to converge on complex pattern structures. A neural network without an activation function is essentially just a linear regression model.

There are a number of different activation functions we can use in our neural networks. A non-exhaustive list of activation functions may be found here:

- Binary Step

- Linear

- Sigmoid (Logistic Activation Function)

- Tanh (Hyperbolic Tangent)

- ReLU (Rectified Linear Unit)

- Softmax

- Leaky ReLU

- Parameterized ReLU

- Exponential Linear Unit

- Swish

Among these activation functions, Tanh, ReLU, and Sigmoid activation functions are widely used for single neuron activation. Also, the Softmax function is widely used after layers. You may find the X-Y plots for Tanh, ReLU, and Sigmoid functions in Figure 3-8.

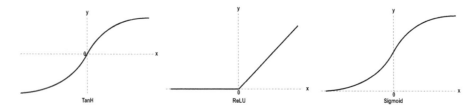

Figure 3-8. *Plots for Tanh, ReLU, and Sigmoid Functions*

Depending on the nature of the problem, one activation function may perform better than the other. Even though ReLU, Tanh, and Sigmoid functions usually converge well in deep learning, we should try all possible functions and optimize our training to achieve the highest accuracy performance possible. A straightforward comparison between ReLU, Tanh, and Sigmoid can be made with the following bullet points:

- ReLU function is a widely used general-purpose activation function. It should be used in hidden layers. In case there are dead neurons, Leaky ReLU may fix potential problems.

- The Sigmoid function works best in classification tasks.

- Sigmoid and Tanh functions may cause vanishing gradient problem.

The best strategy for an optimized training practice is to start with ReLU and try the other activation functions to see if the performance improves.

Loss (Cost or Error) Functions

Loss functions are functions that are used to measure the performance of a deep learning model for given data. It is usually based on error terms, which is calculated as the distance between the real (measured) value and the prediction of the trained model.

$$e_i = y_i - \hat{y}_i$$

Error = Measured Value - Predicted Value

Therefore, we end up with an error term for each prediction we make. Imagine you are working with millions of data points. To be able to derive insights from these individual error terms, we need an aggregative function so that we can come up with a single value for performance evaluation. This function is referred to as **loss function, cost function, or error function, depending on the context**.

Several loss functions are used for performance evaluation, and choosing the right function is an integral part of model building. This selection must be based on the nature of the problem. While Root Mean Squared Error (RMSE) function is the right loss function for regression problems in which we would like to penalize large errors, multi-class crossentropy should be selected for multi-class classification problems.

In addition, to be used to generate a single value for aggregated error terms, the loss function may also be used for rewards in reinforcement learning. In this book, we will mostly use loss functions with error terms, but beware that it is possible to use loss functions as a reward measure.

Several loss functions are used in deep learning tasks. Root mean squared error (RMSE), mean squared error (MSE), mean absolute error (MAE), and mean absolute percentage error (MAPE) are some of the appropriate loss functions for regression problems. For binary and multi-class classification problems, we can use variations of crossentropy (i.e., *logarithmic*) function.

Optimization in Deep Learning

Now that we covered activation and loss functions, it is time to move on to weight and bias optimization. Activation functions used in neurons and layers make final adjustments on the linear results derived from weights and bias terms. We can make predictions using these parameters (weights and biases). The distances between the actual values and the predicted values are recorded as error terms. These error terms are aggregated into a single value with loss functions. In addition to this process, optimization functions make small changes to the weights and biases and measure the effects of these changes with loss functions. This process helps to find the optimal weight and bias values to minimize errors and maximize the accuracy of the model. This training cycle is shown in Figure 3-9.

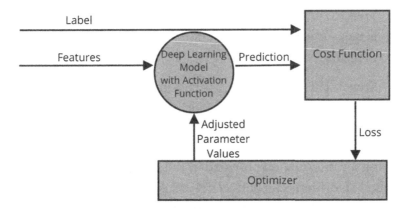

Figure 3-9. *Deep Learning Model Training with Cost Function, Activation Function, and Optimizer*

There are several optimization algorithms and challenges encountered during the optimization process. In this section, we will briefly introduce these functions and challenges. But first, let's take a look at an essential optimization concept: *backpropagation.*

Backpropagation

The backpropagation algorithm is an essential component in neural network architecture used for iteration in parallel with optimizer. It serves as a central mechanism by which neural networks learn. The name explains itself since the word ***propagate*** means to transmit something. Therefore, the word ***backpropagation*** means "*transmitting information back.*" This is what the backpropagation algorithm precisely does: it takes the calculated loss back to the system, which is used by the optimizer to adjust the weights and biases. This process may be explained step by step, as shown here:

- **Step 1**: The trained neural network makes a prediction with the current weights and biases.

- **Step 2**: The performance of the neural network is measured with a loss function as a single error measure.

- **Step 3**: This error measure is backpropagated to optimizer so that it can readjust the weights and biases.

- **Repeat**

By using the information provided by the backpropagation algorithm, optimization algorithms can perfect the weights and biases used in the neural network. Let's take a look at the optimization algorithms (i.e., *optimizers*), which are used in parallel with the backpropagation mechanism.

Optimization Algorithms

An optimization algorithm may be defined as an algorithm helping another algorithm to maximize its performance without delay. Deep learning is one field where optimization algorithms are widely used. The most common optimization algorithms used in deep learning tasks are listed as follows:

- Adam

- Stochastic gradient descent (SGD)

- Adadelta

- Rmsprop

- Adamax

- Adagrad

- Nadam

Note that all of these optimizers are readily available in TensorFlow as well as the loss and activation functions, which are previously mentioned. The most common ones used in real applications are Adam optimizer and Stochastic gradient descent (SGD) optimizer. Let's take a look at the mother of all optimizers, gradient descent and SGD, to have a better understanding of how an optimization algorithm works.

Gradient Descent and Stochastic Gradient Descent (SGD) – Stochastic gradient descent is a variation of gradient descent methods. SGD is widely used as an iterative optimization method in deep learning. The roots of SGD date back to the 1950s, and it is one of the oldest – yet successful – optimization algorithms.

Gradient descent methods are a family of optimization algorithms used to minimize the total loss (or cost) in the neural networks. There are several gradient descent implementations: The original gradient descent – or batch gradient descent – algorithm uses the whole training data per epoch. Stochastic (Random) gradient descent (SGD) selects a random observation to measure the changes in total loss (or cost) as a result of the changes in weights and biases. Finally, mini-batch gradient descent uses a small batch so that training may still be fast as well as reliable.

Epoch   is the hyperparameter that represents the number of times that the values of a neural network are to be adjusted using the training dataset.

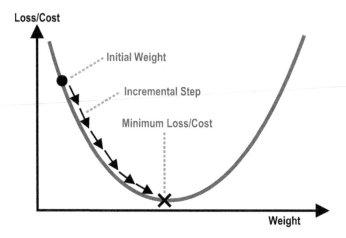

Figure 3-10. *A Weight-Loss Plot Showing Gradient Descent*

Figure 3-10 shows how gradient descent algorithm works. Larger incremental steps are taken when the machine learning expert selects a faster learning rate.

Learning Rate   is the parameter in optimization algorithms which regulates the step size taken at each iteration while moving forward a minimum of a loss/cost function. With a fast learning rate, the model converges around the minimum faster, yet it may overshoot the actual minimum point. With a slow learning rate, optimization may take too much time. Therefore, a machine learning expert must choose the optimal learning rate, which allows the model to find the desired minimum point in a reasonable time.

Adam Optimizer – What Is Adam?

I will not dive into the details of the other optimization algorithms since they are mostly altered or improved implementations of gradient descent methods. Therefore, understanding the gradient descent algorithm will be enough for the time being.

In the next section, we see the optimization challenges which negatively affect the optimization process during training. Some of the optimization algorithms, as mentioned earlier, were developed to mitigate these challenges.

Optimization Challenges

There are three optimization challenges we often encounter in deep learning. These challenges are (i) local minima, (ii) saddle points, and (iii) vanishing gradients. Let's briefly discuss what they are.

Local Minima – In neural network training, a simple loss-weight plot with a single minimum might be useful to visualize the relationship between the weight and the calculated loss for educational purposes. However, in real-world problems, this plot might contain many local minima, and our optimization algorithm may converge on one local minimum rather than the global minimum point. Figure 3-11 shows how our model can be stuck at a local minimum.

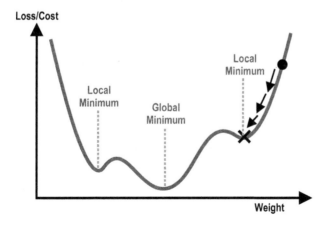

Figure 3-11. *A Weight-Loss Plot with Two Local Minima and a Global Minimum*

Saddle Points – Saddle points are stable points in the graphs that the algorithm cannot figure out whether it is a local minimum or a local maximum. Both sides of a saddle point have zero slopes. Optimizers using more than one observation for loss calculation may be stuck in a saddle point. Therefore, Stochastic gradient descent is a suitable solution for saddle points. A simplified graph with saddle point is shown in Figure 3-12.

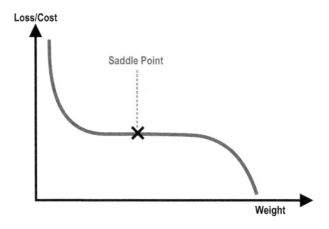

Figure 3-12. *A Weight-Loss Plot with Two Local Minima and a Global Minimum*

Vanishing Gradients – Excessive use of certain activation functions (e.g., Sigmoid) may negatively affect the optimization algorithm. It becomes difficult to reduce the output of the loss function since the gradient of the loss function approaches zero. An effective solution to the vanishing gradient problem is to use ReLU as the activation function in hidden layers. Sigmoid activation function – the main reason for the vanishing gradient problem – and its derivative are shown in Figure 3-13.

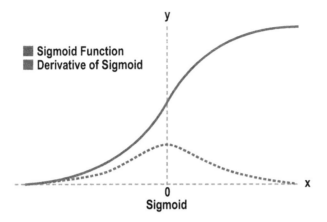

Figure 3-13. *The Sigmoid Function and Its Derivative*

To be able to solve this common optimization challenges, we should try and find the best combination of activation functions and optimization functions so that our model correctly converges and finds an ideal minimum point.

Overfitting and Regularization

Another important concept in deep learning and machine learning is overfitting. In this section, we cover the overfitting problem and how to address overfitting with regularization methods.

Overfitting

In Chapter 2, we already explained the concept of overfitting briefly for machine learning. Overfitting is also a challenge in deep learning. We don't want our neural network to fit a limited set of data points too tightly, which jeopardizes its performance in the real world. We also don't want our model to underfit since it would not give us a good accuracy level. Underfitting and overfitting problems are shown in Figure 3-14.

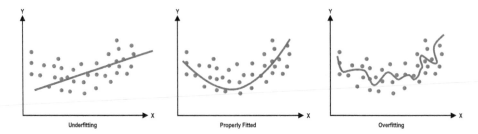

Figure 3-14. *Underfitting and Overfitting in X-Y Plot*

The solution to the underfitting problem is building a good model with meaningful features, feeding enough data, and training enough. On the other hand, more data, removing excessive features, and cross-validation are proper methods to fight the overfitting problem. In addition, we have a group of sophisticated methods to overcome overfitting problems, namely, regularization methods.

Regularization

Regularization is a technique to fight overfitting. There are a number of possible methods used for regularization, which may be listed as follows:

- Early stopping

- Dropout

- L1 and L2 regularization

- Data augmentation

Early Stopping – Early stopping is a very simple – yet effective – strategy to prevent overfitting. Setting a sufficient number of epochs (training steps) is crucial to achieving a good level of accuracy. However, you may easily go overboard and train your model to fit too tightly to your training data. With early stopping, the learning algorithm is stopped if the model does not show a significant performance improvement for a certain number of epochs.

Dropout – Dropout is another simple – yet effective – regularization method. With dropout enabled, our model temporarily removes some of the neurons or layers from the network, which adds additional noise to the neural network. This noise prevents the model from fitting to the training data too closely and makes the model more flexible.

L1 and L2 Regularization – These two methods add an additional penalty term to the loss function, which penalizes the errors even more. For L1 regularization, this term is a lasso regression, whereas it is ridge regression for L2 regularization. L1 and L2 regularizations are particularly helpful when dealing with a large set of features.

Data Augmentation – Data augmentation is a method to increase the amount of training data. By making small transformations on the existing data, we can generate more observations and add them to the original dataset. Data augmentation increases the total amount of training data, which helps preventing the overfitting problem.

Feature Scaling

Another crucial concept in deep learning is feature scaling. Feature scaling is a method to normalize the range of features so that neural networks perform more accurately. When the range of the values of a feature varies considerably, some objective functions may not work correctly in machine learning models. For instance, classifiers usually calculate the distance between two data points. When the variance of the values of a feature is large, this feature dictates this calculated distance, which means **an inflated influence of this particular feature on the outcome**. Scaling the value ranges of each feature helps to eliminate this problem. There are several feature scaling methods which are listed as follows:

- **Standardization**: It adjusts the values of each feature to have zero mean and unit variance.

- **Min-Max Normalization (Rescaling)**: It scales the values of each feature between [0, 1] and [-1, 1].

- **Mean Normalization**: It deducts the mean from each data point and divides the result to max-min differential. It is a slightly altered and less popular version of min-max normalization.

- **Scaling to Unit Length**: It divides each component of a feature by the Euclidian length of the vector of this feature.

Using feature scaling has two benefits in deep learning:

- It ensures that each feature contributes to the prediction algorithm proportionately.

- It speeds up the convergence of the gradient descent algorithm, which reduces the time required for training a model.

Final Evaluations

In this chapter, we covered the timeline of artificial neural networks and deep learning. It helped us to understand how the concepts we use in our professional lives came to life after many years of research. The good news is that thanks to TensorFlow, we are able to add these components in our neural networks in a matter of seconds.

Following the deep learning timeline, we analyzed the structure of neural networks and the artificial neurons in detail. Also, we covered the fundamental deep learning concepts, including (i) optimization functions, (ii) activation functions, (iii) loss functions, (iv) overfitting and regularization, and (v) feature scaling.

This chapter serves as a continuation of the previous chapter where we cover the machine learning basics. In the next chapter, we learn about the most popular complementary technologies used in deep learning studies: (i) NumPy, (ii) SciPy, (iii) Matplotlib, (iii) Pandas, (iv) scikit-learn, and (v) Flask.

CHAPTER 4

Complementary Libraries to TensorFlow 2.x

Now that we covered the basics of machine learning and deep learning, we can slowly move on to the applied side of deep learning. As you know, every machine learning application, including deep learning applications, has a pipeline consisting of several steps. TensorFlow offers us several modules for all these steps. Even though TensorFlow is very powerful for model building, training, evaluation, and making predictions, we still need other complementary libraries for certain tasks, especially for data preparation. Although the potential libraries you may use in a deep learning pipeline may vary to a great extent, the most popular complementary libraries are as follows:

- NumPy
- SciPy
- Pandas
- Matplotlib
- Scikit-learn
- Flask

© Orhan Gazi Yalçın 2021
O. G. Yalçın, *Applied Neural Networks with TensorFlow 2*,
https://doi.org/10.1007/978-1-4842-6513-0_4

Especially after TensorFlow 2.x, we started to see more and more data preparation, visualization, and other relevant capabilities added to TensorFlow. However, these capabilities cannot yet be compared to what these dedicated libraries have to offer. Table 4-1 lists these libraries with their core capabilities.

Table 4-1. *The Libraries Complementary to TensorFlow and Their Main Use Cases*

Library	Core Capability
NumPy	Array processing
SciPy	Scientific computing
Pandas	Array processing and data analysis including data visualization
Matplotlib	Data visualization
Scikit-learn	Machine learning
Flask	Web framework for deployment

Let's take a look at how to install them all together using pip, our package installer for Python.

Installation with Pip

Pip is the *de facto* standard package-management system for Python, and it is already included in the Python installation package. You can easily install and manage Python libraries with ***pip***.

The original environments to use ***pip*** are Terminal for macOS and Command Prompt for Windows OS. However, you can also use ***pip*** inside Jupyter Notebook and Google Colab with a small adjustment. The difference between these two options is only an exclamation mark (!).

Terminal and Command Prompt	Jupyter Notebook and Google Colab
pip install *package-name*	!pip install *package-name*

If you decide to follow this book with your local Jupyter Notebook installation, we have to make sure that you have pip installed on your system.

Use of Pip in Google Colab If you are using Google Colab as recommended, you don't have to worry about whether you have pip on your system. You can use pip inside your Google Colab Notebook with an exclamation mark.

Pip installation, *or its confirmation,* can be achieved in three steps:

1. Open Terminal for macOS/Command Prompt for Windows OS:

   a. You can open a Terminal window from Launchpad under Others folder.

   b. You can open a Command Line window by (i) pressing Windows+X to open the Power Users menu and then (ii) clicking "Command Prompt" or "Command Prompt (Admin)."

2. Check if **pip** installed and view the current version installed on your system with the following script:

   pip --version

3. If Terminal/Command Line does not return version info, install pip with the following command:
   python -m pip install -U pip

If it returns version info, then you confirm that you have pip installed on your system.

4. Close the Terminal/Command Line window.

Installation of the Libraries – Now that we confirmed you have pip on your system, you can install all the aforementioned libraries in this chapter with the following scripts in Table 4-2.

Table 4-2. *The Complementary Libraries with Pip Installation Scripts*

Library	Installation Script
NumPy	`pip install numpy`
SciPy	`pip install scipy`
Pandas	`pip install pandas`
Matplotlib	`pip install matplotlib`
Scikit-learn	`pip install scikit-learn`
Flask	`pip install flask`

Beware of Already Installed Packages Both Google Colab Notebooks and Jupyter Notebooks already come with most of these libraries preinstalled. Just run the scripts mentioned earlier once to make sure you have them installed so that you won't be bothered during case studies in case some of them are missing.

Now that we are sure that you have these libraries installed in your system (either Google Colab or Jupyter Notebook), we can dive into details of these libraries.

NumPy – Array Processing

 NumPy (Numerical Python) is a very popular open-source numerical Python library, created by Travis Oliphant. NumPy provides multidimensional arrays along with a significant number of useful functions for mathematical operations.

NumPy acts as a wrapper around the corresponding library implemented in C. Therefore, it offers the best of two worlds: (i) efficiency of C and (ii) ease of use of Python. NumPy arrays are easy-to-create and efficient objects for (i) storing data and (ii) fast matrix operations. With NumPy, you can quickly generate arrays with random numbers, which is perfect for an enhanced learning experience and proof of concept tasks. Also, the Pandas library, which we will cover later on, heavily relies on NumPy objects and almost works as a NumPy extension.

Thanks to NumPy arrays, we can process data in large volumes and do advanced mathematical operations with ease. Compared to built-in Python sequences, NumPy's ndarray object executes much faster and more efficient with less code. There are a growing number of libraries that rely on NumPy arrays for processing data, which shows the power of NumPy. Since deep learning models are usually trained with millions of data points, size and speed superiority of NumPy arrays are essential for the machine learning experts.

Useful Information About NumPy

- **Website**: www.numpy.org/

- **Documentation URL**: https://numpy.org/doc/

- **Installation Command**: pip install numpy

- **Preferred Alias for Importing**: import numpy as np

SciPy – Scientific Computing

 SciPy is an open-source Python library that contains a collection of functions used for mathematical, scientific, and engineering studies. SciPy functions are built on the NumPy library. SciPy allows users to manipulate and visualize their data with an easy-to-use syntax. SciPy is a library that boosts developers' data processing and system-prototyping capabilities and makes Python as effective as the rival systems such as MATLAB, IDL, Octave, R-Lab, and SciLab. Therefore, SciPy's collection of data processing and prototyping functions strengthens Python's already established superiority as a general-purpose programming language even further.

SciPy's vast collection of functions is organized into domain-based sub-packages. SciPy sub-packages must be called separately from the mother SciPy library such as

```
from scipy import stats, special
```

In Table 4-3, you may find a list of SciPy sub-packages.

Table 4-3. *SciPy Sub-packages*

Sub-package	Description	Sub-package	Description
stats	Statistical functions and distributions	linalg	Linear algebra
special	Special functions	io	Input and output
spatial	Spatial data structures and algorithms	interpolate	Interpolation and smoothing splines
sparse	Sparse matrices and associated routines	integrate	Integration and equation solving
signal	Signal processing	fftpack	Fast Fourier transform routines
optimize	Optimization and root-finding routines	constants	Physical and mathematical constants
odr	Orthogonal distance regression	cluster	Clustering algorithms
ndimage	N-dimensional image processing		

Useful Information About SciPy

- **Website**: https://www.scipy.org/scipylib/

- **Documentation URL**: https://docs.scipy.org/doc/

- **Installation Command**: pip install scipy

- **Preferred Alias for Importing**: from scipy import *sub-package-name*

Pandas – Array Processing and Data Analysis

 Pandas is a Python library that offers flexible and expressive data structures suitable for performing fast mathematical operations. Python is a comprehensive and easy-to-use data analysis library, and it aims to become the leading open-source language-neutral data analysis tool.

One-dimensional Series and two-dimensional DataFrames are the two main data structures in pandas. Since it extends the capabilities of NumPy and it is built on top of NumPy, Pandas almost operates as a NumPy extension. Pandas also offers several data visualization methods, which are very useful to derive insights from the datasets.

You can analyze your data and perform several calculation tasks with Pandas. Here is a non-exhaustive list of the things you can do with Pandas:

- Handling missing data by filling and dropping

- Data insertion and deletion thanks to allowed mutability

- Automatic and explicit data alignment

- Group-by and order-by functionality

- Easily converting unorganized objects to DataFrames

- Slice, index, and subset operations

- Merge, concatenate, and join operations

- Reshape and pivot operations

- Hierarchical and multiple labeling

- Specific operations for time-series and sequence data

- Robust input and output operations with extensive file format support (including CSV, XLSX, HTML, HDF5)

Since Pandas is a *de facto* extension of NumPy, which improves its capabilities, we take advantage of Pandas more often than NumPy. But there are cases where we have to rely on NumPy due to limitations of other complementary libraries.

Useful Information About Pandas

- **Website**: https://pandas.pydata.org/

- **Documentation URL**: https://pandas.pydata.org/ docs/

- **Installation Command**: pip install pandas

- **Preferred Alias for Importing:** import pandas as pd

Matplotlib and Seaborn – Data Visualization

 Matplotlib is a Python data visualization library for creating static, animated, and interactive graphs and plots. You can produce high-quality plots for academic publications, blogs, and books, and you can also derive insights from large datasets using Matplotlib.

In addition to deriving insights with your Google Colab Notebook, you can also use the object-oriented API of Matplotlib for embedding plots into applications. The three main functionalities of Matplotlib can be listed as follows:

- **Create**: With Matplotlib, you can create high-quality plots with a minimal amount of code. The total number of graph types offered by Matplotlib exceeds hundreds – from histograms to heat plots, from bar charts to surface plots.

- **Customize**: Matplotlib plots are flexible in the sense that you can customize line styles, font properties, colors, and axes information. You can export from your plot and embed data into your plot.

- **Extend**: You can take advantage of numerous third-party libraries extending Matplotlib. Some of these libraries are also extremely useful, such as **_Seaborn_**.

The things you can do with Matplotlib may be listed as follows:

- Use PyPlot module and create interactive plots.

- Create hundreds of different graphs and plots using lines, bars, markers, and other objects.

- Create unique plots such as surface and contours plots.

- Add images and fields to your plots.

- Create multiple subplots under a single figure.

- Flexibly edit text, axes, colors, labels, and annotations in a plot.

- Create one or more shapes with Matplotlib.

- Create showcase figures.

- Take advantage of the animation support.

Useful Information About Matplotlib

- **Website**: https://matplotlib.org/

- **Documentation URL**: https://matplotlib.org/3.2.1/
  contents.html (make sure you enter the latest version)

- **Installation Command:** pip install matplotlib

- **Preferred Alias for Importing:** import matplotlib.
  pyplot as plt

seaborn

Besides vanilla Matplotlib, third-party packages are widely used for increasing the capabilities of Matplotlib. One of the useful data visualization libraries built on top of Matplotlib is Seaborn. Seaborn is a data visualization library based on Matplotlib. It provides a high-level interface for extending the capabilities of Matplotlib. You can reduce the time required to generate insightful graphs with Seaborn.

Useful Information About Seaborn

- **Website**: https://seaborn.pydata.org/

- **Gallery**: https://seaborn.pydata.org/examples/

- **Installation Command:** pip install seaborn

- **Preferred Alias for Importing:** import seaborn as sns

Scikit-learn – Machine Learning

Scikit-learn is a powerful open-source machine learning library for Python, initially developed by David Cournapeau as a Google Summer of Code project. You can use scikit-learn as a stand-alone machine learning library and successfully build a wide range of traditional machine learning models. Besides being able to create machine learning models, scikit-learn, which is built on top of NumPy, SciPy, and Matplotlib, provides simple and efficient tools for predictive data analysis. There are six main functionalities of scikit-learn, which are listed as follows:

- **Classification**: Scikit-learn offers several algorithms to identify which category an object belongs to, such as support vector machines, logistic regression, k-nearest neighbors, decision trees, and many more.

- **Regression**: Several algorithms offered by scikit-learn can predict a continuous-valued response variable associated with an object such as linear regression, gradient boosting, random forest, decision trees, and many more.

- **Clustering**: Scikit-learn also offers clustering algorithms, which are used for automated grouping of similar objects into clusters, such as k-means clustering, spectral clustering, mean shift, and many more.

- **Dimensionality Reduction**: Scikit-learn provides several algorithms to reduce the number of explanatory variables to consider, such as PCA, feature selection, nonnegative matrix factorization, and many more.

- **Model Selection**: Scikit-learn can help with model validation and comparison, and also it can help choose parameters and models. You can compare your TensorFlow models with scikit-learn's traditional machine learning models. Grid search, cross-validation, and metrics are some of the tools used for model selection and validation functionality.

- **Preprocessing**: With preprocessing, feature extraction, and feature scaling options, you can transform your data where TensorFlow falls short.

Scikit-learn is especially useful when we want to compare our deep learning models with other machine learning algorithms. In addition, with scikit-learn, we can preprocess our data before feeding it into our deep learning pipeline.

Useful Information About Scikit-learn

- **Website**: https://scikit-learn.org/

- **User Guide**: https://scikit-learn.org/stable/ user_guide.html

- **Installation Command**: pip install scikit-learn

- **Preferred Alias for Importing:** from scikit-learn import *

Flask – Deployment

 As opposed to the libraries mentioned earlier, Flask is not a data science library, but it is a micro web framework for Python. It is considered as a microframework because it is not packaged with the components that the other web frameworks deem essential such as database abstraction layer and form validation. These components can be embedded in a Flask application with powerful third-party extensions. This characteristic makes Flask simple and lightweighted and reduces development time. Flask is a perfect option if you want to serve your trained deep learning models, and you don't want to spend too much time on web programming.

Flask is easy to learn and to implement as opposed to Django. Django is a very well-documented and a popular web framework for Python. But due to its large size with a lot of built-in extension packages, Django would be a better choice for large projects. Currently, Flask has more stars on its GitHub repo than any other web framework for Python and voted the most popular web framework in the Python Developers Survey 2018.

Useful Information About Flask

- **Website**: https://palletsprojects.com/p/flask/

- **Documentation URL**: https://flask.
  palletsprojects.com/

- **Installation Command**: pip install flask

- **Preferred Alias for Importing**: from flask import
  Flask, *

Final Evaluations

In this chapter, we make an introduction to the most commonly
used libraries complementary to TensorFlow. We predominantly use
TensorFlow thanks to its growing number of modules addressing the needs
of developers at every step of the pipeline. However, there are still some
operations we have to rely on these libraries.

While NumPy and Pandas are very powerful data processing libraries,
Matplotlib and Seaborn are useful for data visualization. While SciPy helps
us with complex mathematical operations, scikit-learn is particularly
useful for advanced preprocessing operations and validation tasks. Finally,
Flask is the web framework of our choice to serve our trained models
quickly.

In the next chapter, we dive into TensorFlow modules with actual code
examples.

## CHAPTER 5

A Guide to TensorFlow 2.0 and Deep Learning Pipeline

In the previous chapters, we cover the fundamentals before diving into deep learning applications.

- Chapter 1 is useful to understand the reasons behind the selection of technologies such as Python and TensorFlow. It also helped us setting up our environments.

- Chapter 2 makes a brief introduction to machine learning since deep learning is a subfield of machine learning.

- In Chapter 3, we finally cover the basics of deep learning. These three chapters were conceptual and introductory chapters.

- Chapter 4 summarizes all the technologies we use in our deep learning pipeline, except for one: TensorFlow.

© Orhan Gazi Yalçın 2021
O. G. Yalçın, *Applied Neural Networks with TensorFlow 2*,
https://doi.org/10.1007/978-1-4842-6513-0_5

In this chapter, we cover the basics of TensorFlow and the API references that we use in this book.

TensorFlow Basics

The main focus of this chapter is how we can use TensorFlow for neural networks and model training, but first, we need to cover a few topics under TensorFlow Basics, which are

- Eager execution vs. graph execution

- TensorFlow constants

- TensorFlow variables

Eager Execution

One of the novelties brought with TensorFlow 2.0 was to make the eager execution the default option. With eager execution, TensorFlow calculates the values of tensors as they occur in your code. Eager execution simplifies the model building experience in TensorFlow, and you can see the result of a TensorFlow operation instantly.

The main motivation behind this change of heart was PyTorch's dynamic computational graph capability. With the dynamic computational graph capability, PyTorch users were able to follow *define-by-run* approach, in which you can see the result of an operation instantly.

However, with graph execution, TensorFlow 1.x followed a *define-and-run* approach, in which evaluation happens only after we've wrapped our code with `tf.Session`. Graph execution has advantages for distributed training, performance optimizations, and production deployment. But graph execution also drove the newcomers away to PyTorch due to the difficulty of implementation. Therefore, this difficulty for newcomers led the TensorFlow team to adopt eager execution, TensorFlow's *define-by-run* approach, as the default execution method.

In this book, we only use the default eager execution for model building and training.

Tensor

Tensors are TensorFlow's built-in multidimensional arrays with uniform type. They are very similar to NumPy arrays, and they are immutable, which means that once created, they cannot be altered, and you can only create a new copy with the edits.

Tensors are categorized based on the number of dimensions they have:

- **Rank-0 (Scalar) Tensor**: A tensor containing a single value and no axes

- **Rank-1 Tensor**: A tensor containing a list of values in a single axis

- **Rank-2 Tensor**: A tensor containing two axes

- **Rank-N Tensor**: A tensor containing N-axis

For example, a Rank-3 Tensor can be created and printed out with the following lines:

```
rank_3_tensor = tf.constant([
  [[0, 1, 2, 3, 4],
   [5, 6, 7, 8, 9]],
  [[10, 11, 12, 13, 14],
   [15, 16, 17, 18, 19]],
  [[20, 21, 22, 23, 24],
   [25, 26, 27, 28, 29]],])

print(rank_3_tensor)
```

You can access detailed information about the tf.Tensor object with the following functions:

```
print("Type of every element:", rank_3_tensor.dtype)
print("Number of dimensions:", rank_3_tensor.ndim)
print("Shape of tensor:", rank_3_tensor.shape)
print("Elements along axis 0 of tensor:", rank_3_tensor.
shape[0])
print("Elements along the last axis of tensor:", rank_3_tensor.
shape[-1])
print("Total number of elements (3*2*5): ", tf.size(rank_3_
tensor).numpy())
```
Output:
```
Type of every element: <dtype: 'int32'>
Number of dimensions: 3
Shape of tensor: (3, 2, 5)
Elements along axis 0 of tensor: 3
Elements along the last axis of tensor: 5
Total number of elements (3*2*5):   30
```

There are several functions that create a Tensor object. Other than tf. Constant(), we often use tf.ones() and tf.zeros() functions to create tensors with only ones or zeros of given size. The following lines provide example for both:

```
zeros = tf.zeros(shape=[2,3])
print(zeros)
```
Output:
```
tf.Tensor(
[[0. 0. 0.]
 [0. 0. 0.]], shape=(2, 3), dtype=float32)
```
```
ones = tf.ones(shape=[2,3])
print(ones)
```
Output:
```
tf.Tensor(
```

```
[[1. 1. 1.]
 [1. 1. 1.]], shape=(2, 3), dtype=float32)
```

The base `tf.Tensor` class requires tensors to be in a rectangular shape, which means along each axis, every element has the same size. However, there are specialized types of tensors that can handle different shapes:

- **Ragged Tensors**: A tensor with variable numbers of elements along some axis

- **Sparse Tensors**: A tensor where our data is sparse, like a very wide embedding space

Variable

A TensorFlow variable is the recommended way to represent a shared, persistent state that you can manipulate with a model. TensorFlow variables are recorded as a `tf.Variable` object. A `tf.Variable` object represents a tensor whose values can be changed, as opposed to plain TensorFlow constants. `tf.Variable` objects are used to store model parameters.

TensorFlow variables are very similar to TensorFlow constants, with one significant difference: variables are mutable. So, the values of a variable object can be altered (e.g., with `assign()` function) as well as the shape of the variable object (e.g., with `reshape()` function).

You can create a basic variable with the following code:

```
a = tf.Variable([2.0, 3.0])
```

You can also use an existing constant to create a variable:

```
my_tensor = tf.constant([[1.0, 2.0], [3.0, 4.0]])
my_variable = tf.Variable(my_tensor)
print(my_variable)
```
Output:

```
<tf.Variable 'Variable:0' shape=(2, 2) dtype=float32, numpy=
array([[1., 2.],
       [3., 4.]], dtype=float32)>
```

You can convert a TensorFlow variable object or a TensorFlow tensor object to a NumPy array with the `tensor.numpy()` function, as shown here:

```
my_variable.numpy()
my_tensor.numpy()
```

These are some of the fundamental concepts in TensorFlow. Now we can move on to the model building and data processing with TensorFlow.

TensorFlow Deep Learning Pipeline

In the last section of Chapter 2, we listed the steps of a complete machine learning pipeline (i.e., steps to obtain a trained machine learning model). In deep learning models, we almost exclusively use the same pipeline, in which there is a great deal of work for TensorFlow. Figure 5-1 shows how our pipeline works (please note that you may encounter slight alterations in different sources).

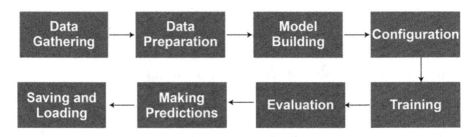

Figure 5-1. *Deep Learning Pipeline Built with TensorFlow*

In the next sections, we cover these steps with code examples. Please note that the data gathering step will be omitted since it is usually regarded as a separate task and not usually performed by machine learning experts.

Data Loading and Preparation

Before building and training a neural network, the first step to deep learning is to load your data, process it, and feed it to the neural network. All the neural networks we cover in the next chapters require data, and for this, we need to feed the data in the right format. Our TensorFlow model accepts several object types, which can be listed as follows:

- TensorFlow Dataset object

- TensorFlow Datasets catalog

- NumPy array object

- Pandas DataFrame object

Let's dive into how we can use them.

Dataset Object (tf.data.Dataset)

TensorFlow Dataset object represents a large set of elements (i.e., a dataset). `tf.data.Dataset` API is one of the objects TensorFlow accepts as model input used for training and specifically designed for input pipelines.

You can use the Dataset API with the following purposes:

- Create a dataset from the given data.

- Transform the dataset with collective functions such as map.

- Iterate over the dataset and process individual elements.

Dataset API supports various file formats and Python objects, which can be used to create `tf.data.Dataset` objects. Let's take a look at some of these supported file formats and objects:

- Dataset from a Python list, NumPy array, Pandas DataFrame with `from_tensor_slices` function

```
ds = tf.data.Dataset.from_tensor_slices([1, 2, 3])
ds = tf.data.Dataset.from_tensor_slices(numpy_array)
ds = tf.data.Dataset.from_tensor_slices(df.values)
```

- Dataset from a text file with `TextLineDataset` function

```
ds = tf.data.TextLineDataset("file.txt")
```

- Dataset from TensorFlow's TFRecord format with `TFRecordDataset` function

```
ds = tf.data.TFRecordDataset("file.tfrecord")
```

- Dataset from CSV file with

```
ds = tf.data.experimental.make_csv_dataset
( "file.csv", batch_size=5)
```

- Dataset from TensorFlow Datasets catalog: This will be covered in the next section.

TensorFlow Datasets Catalog

TensorFlow Datasets is a collection of popular datasets that are maintained by TensorFlow. They are usually clean and ready to use.

Installation

TensorFlow Datasets exists in two packages:

- `tensorflow-datasets`: The stable version, updated every few months

- `tfds-nightly`: The nightly released version, which contains the latest versions of the datasets

As you can understand from the names, you may use either the stable version, which updates less frequently but is more reliable, or the nightly released version, which gives access to the latest versions of the dataset. But beware that because of the frequent releases, `tfds-nightly` is more prone to breaking and, thus, is not recommended to be used in production-level projects.

In case you don't have it on your systems, you may install these packages with the following command-line scripts:

```
pip install tensorflow_datasets
pip install tfds-nightly
```

Importing

These packages are loaded via `tensorflow_datasets`, which is usually abbreviated as `tfds`. To be able to import these packages, all you have to do is to run a single line, as shown here:

```
import tensorflow_datasets as tfds
```

Datasets Catalog

After the main library is imported, we can use load function to import one of the popular libraries listed in the TensorFlow Datasets catalog page, which is accessible on

`www.tensorflow.org/datasets/catalog/overview`

Under this catalog, you may find dozens of datasets, which belong to one of these listed groups:

- Audio
- Image
- Image classification
- Object detection

- Question answering

- Structured

- Summarization

- Text

- Translate

- Video

Loading a Dataset

The easiest way to load a dataset from TensorFlow Datasets catalog is to use the load function. This function will

- Download the dataset.

- Save it as TFRecord files.

- Load the TFRecord files to your notebook.

- Create a tf.data.Dataset object, which can be used to train a model.

The following example shows how to load a dataset with the load function:

```
mnist_dataset = tfds.load('mnist', split='train')
```

You can customize your loading process by setting particular arguments of your load function:

- **split**: Controls which part of the dataset to load

- **shuffle_files**: Controls whether to shuffle the files between each epoch

- **data_dir**: Controls the location where the dataset is saved

- **with_info**: Controls whether the DatasetInfo object will be loaded or not

In our upcoming sections, we take advantage of this catalog to a great extent.

Keras Datasets

In addition to the TensorFlow Datasets catalog, Keras also provides access to a limited number of datasets that are listed in their catalog, accessible on https://keras.io/api/datasets/. The datasets accessible under this catalog are

- MNIST

- CIFAR10

- CIFAR100

- IMDB Movie Reviews

- Reuters Newswire

- Fashion MNIST

- Boston Housing

As you can see, this catalog is very limited, but come in handy in your research projects.

You can load a dataset from Keras API with the load_data() function, as shown here:

```
(x_train, y_train), (x_test, y_test)= tf.keras.datasets.mnist.
load_data( path="mnist.npz" )
```

One important difference of Keras's datasets from TensorFlow's datasets is that they are imported as NumPy array objects.

NumPy Array

One of the data types which are accepted by TensorFlow as input data is NumPy arrays. As mentioned in the previous chapter, you can import NumPy library with the following line:

```
import numpy as np
```

You can create a NumPy array with `np.array()` function, which can be fed into the TensorFlow model. You can also use a function such as `np.genfromtxt()` to load a dataset from a CSV file.

In reality, we rarely use a NumPy function to load data. For this task, we often take advantage of the Pandas library, which acts almost as a NumPy extension.

Pandas DataFrame

Pandas DataFrame and Series objects are also accepted by TensorFlow as well as NumPy arrays. There is a strong connection between Pandas and NumPy. To process and clean our data, Pandas often provides more powerful functionalities. However, NumPy arrays are usually more efficient and recognized by other libraries to a greater extent. For example, you may need to use scikit-learn to preprocess your data. Scikit-learn would accept a Pandas DataFrame as well as a NumPy array, but only returns a NumPy array. Therefore, a machine learning expert must learn to use both libraries.

You may import the Pandas libraries, as shown here:

```
import pandas as pd
```

You can easily load datasets from the files in different formats such as CSV, Excel, and text, as shown here:

- **CSV Files**: `pd.read_csv("path/xyz.csv")`

- **Excel Files**: `pd.read_excel("path/xyz.xlsx")`

- **Text Files**: `pd.read_csv("path/xyz.txt")`

- **HTML Files**: `pd.read_html("path/xyz.html")` or `pd.read_html('URL')`

After loading your dataset from these different file formats, Pandas gives you an impressive number of different functionalities, and you can also check the result of your data processing operation with `pandas.DataFrame.head()` or `pandas.DataFrame.tail()` functions.

Other Objects

The number of supported file formats is increasing with the new versions of TensorFlow. In addition, TensorFlow I/O is an extension library that extends the number of supported libraries even further with its API. Although the supported objects and file formats we covered earlier are more than enough, if you are interested in other formats, you may visit TensorFlow I/O's official GitHub repository at

TensorFlow I/O: `https://github.com/tensorflow/io#tensorflow-io`

Model Building

After loading and processing the dataset, the next step is to build a deep learning model to train. We have two major options to build models:

- Keras API

- Estimator API

In this book, we only use Keras API and, therefore, focus on the different ways of building models with Keras API.

Keras API

As mentioned in the earlier chapters, Keras acts as a complementary library to TensorFlow. Also, TensorFlow – with version 2.0 – adopted Keras as a built-in API to build models and for additional functionalities.

Keras API under TensorFlow 2.x provides three different methods to implement neural network models:

- Sequential API

- Functional API

- Model Subclassing

Let's take a look at each method in the following.

Sequential API

The Keras Sequential API allows you to build a neural network step-by-step fashion. You can create a `Sequential()` model object, and you can add a layer at each line.

Using the Keras Sequential API is the easiest method to build models which comes at a cost: *limited customization*. Although you can build a Sequential model within seconds, Sequential models do not provide some of the functionalities such as (i) layer sharing, (ii) multiple branches, (iii) multiple inputs, and (iv) multiple outputs. A Sequential model is the best option when we have a plain stack of layers with one input tensor and one output tensor.

Using the Keras Sequential API is the most basic method to build neural networks, which is sufficient for many of the upcoming chapters. But, to build more complex models, we need to use Keras Functional API and Model Subclassing options.

Building a basic feedforward neural network with the Keras Sequential API can be achieved with the following lines:

```
model = Sequential()
model.add(Flatten(input_shape=(28, 28)))
model.add(Dense(128,'relu'))
model.add(Dense(10, "softmax"))
```

Alternatively, we may just pass a list of layers to the Sequential constructor:

```
model = Sequential([
    Flatten(input_shape=(28, 28)),
    Dense(128,'relu'),
    Dense(10, "softmax"),
  ])
```

Once a Sequential model is built, it behaves like a Functional API model, which provides an input attribute and an output attribute for each layer.

During our case studies, we take advantage of other attributes and functions such as model.layers and model.summary() to understand the structure of our neural network.

Functional API

The Keras Functional API is a more robust and slightly more complex API to build powerful neural networks with TensorFlow. The models we create with the Keras Functional API is inherently more flexible than the models we create with the Keras Sequential API. They can handle nonlinear topology, share layers, and can have multiple branches, inputs, and outputs.

The Keras Functional API methodology stems from the fact that most neural networks are directed acyclic graph (DAG) of layers. Therefore, the Keras team develops Keras Functional API to design this structure. The Keras Functional API is a good way to build graphs of layers.

To create a neural network with the Keras Functional API, we create an input layer and connect it to the first layer. The next layer is connected to the previous one and so on and so forth. Finally, a Model object takes the input and the connected stack of layers as parameters.

The example model in the Keras Sequential API may be constructed using the Keras Functional API as follows:

```
inputs = tf.keras.Input(shape=(28, 28))
x = Flatten()(inputs)
x = Dense(128, "relu")(x)
outputs = Dense(10, "softmax")(x)
model = tf.keras.Model(inputs=inputs,
                       outputs=outputs,
                       name="mnist_model")
```

Just as in the Keras Sequential API, we can use layers attribute, summary() function. In addition, we may also plot the model as a graph with the following line:

```
tf.keras.utils.plot_model(model)
```

Model and Layer Subclassing

Model Subclassing is the most advanced Keras method, which gives us unlimited flexibility to build a neural network from scratch. You can also use Layer Subclassing to build custom layers (i.e., the building blocks of a model) which you can use in a neural network model.

With Model Subclassing, we can build custom-made neural networks to train. Inside of Keras Model class is the root class used to define a model architecture.

The upside of the Model Subclassing is that it's fully customizable, whereas its downside is the difficulty of implementation. Therefore, if you are trying to build exotic neural networks or conducting research-level studies, the Model Subclassing method is the way to go. However, if you can do your project with the Keras Sequential API or the Keras Functional API, you should not bother yourself with the Model Subclassing.

The preceding example you see can be rewritten with Model Subclassing as follows:

```python
class CustomModel(tf.keras.Model):
  def __init__(self, **kwargs):
    super(CustomModel, self).__init__(**kwargs)
    self.layer_1 = Flatten()
    self.layer_2 = Dense(128, "relu")
    self.layer_3 = Dense(10, "softmax")

  def call(self, inputs):
    x = self.layer_1(inputs)
    x = self.layer_2(x)
    x = self.layer_3(x)
    return x

model = CustomModel(name=' mnist_model')
```

There are two crucial functions in Model Subclassing:

- the __init__ function acts as a constructor. Thanks to __init__, we can initialize the attributes (e.g., layers) of our model.

- the super function is used to call the parent constructor (tf.keras.Model).

- the self object is used to refer to instance attributes (e.g., layers).

- the call function is where the operations are defined after the layers are defined in the __init__ function.

In the preceding example, we defined our Dense layers under the __init__ function, then created them as objects, and built our model similar to how we build a neural network using the Keras Functional API. But note that you can build your model in Model Subclassing however you want.

We can complete our model building by generating an object using our custom class (custom model) as follows:

```
model = CustomModel(name='mnist_model')
```

We use Model Subclassing in Chapters 10 and 11.

Estimator API

Estimator API is a high-level TensorFlow API, which encapsulates the following functionalities:

- Training

- Evaluation

- Prediction

- Export for serving

We can take advantage of various premade Estimators as well as we can write our own model with the Estimator API. Estimator API has a few advantages over Keras APIs, such as parameter server-based training and full TFX integration. However, Keras APIs will soon become capable of these functionalities, which makes Estimator API optional.

This book does not cover the Estimator API in case studies. Therefore, we don't go into the details. But, if you are interested in learning more about the Estimator API, please visit the TensorFlow's Guide on Estimator API at www.tensorflow.org/guide/estimator.

Compiling, Training, and Evaluating the Model and Making Predictions

Compiling is an import part of the deep learning model training where we define our (i) optimizer, (ii) loss function, and other parameters such as (iii) callbacks. Training, on the other hand, is the step we start feeding input data into our model so that the model can learn to infer patterns hidden in our dataset. Evaluating is the step where we check our model for common deep learning issues such as overfitting.

There are two methods to compile, train, and evaluate our model:

- Using the standard method

- Writing a custom training loop

The Standard Method

When we follow the standard training method, we can benefit from the following functions:

- `model.compile()`

- `model.fit()`

- `model.evaluate()`

- `model.predict()`

model.compile()

`model.compile()` is the function we set our optimizer, loss function, and performance metrics before training. It is a very straightforward step that can be achieved with a single line of code. Also, note that there are two ways to pass loss function and optimizer arguments within the `model.compile()` function, which may be exemplified as follows:

113

- **Option 1**: Passing arguments as a string

```
model.compile(
optimizer='adam',
loss=mse,
metrics=['accuracy'])
```

- **Option 2**: Passing arguments as a TensorFlow object

```
model.compile(
optimizer=tf.keras.optimizers.Adam() ,
loss=tf.keras.losses.MSE(),
metrics=[tf.keras.metrics.Accuracy()])
```

Passing loss function, metrics, and optimizer as object offers more flexibility than Option 1 since we can also set arguments within the object.

Optimizer

The optimizer algorithms supported by TensorFlow are as follows:

- Adadelta
- Adagrad
- Adam
- Adamax
- Ftrl
- Nadam
- RMSProp
- SGD

The up-to-date list can be found at this URL:

www.tensorflow.org/api_docs/python/tf/keras/optimizers

You may select an optimizer via tf.keras.optimizers module.

Loss Function

Another important argument, which must be set, before starting the training is the loss function. tf.keras.losses module supports a number of loss functions suitable for classification and regression tasks. The entire list can be found at this URL:

www.tensorflow.org/api_docs/python/tf/keras/losses

model.fit()

model.fit() trains the model for a fixed number of epochs (iterations on a dataset). It takes several arguments such as epochs, callbacks, and shuffle, but it must also take another argument: our data. Depending on the problem, this data might be (i) features only or (ii) features and labels. An example usage of the model.fit() function is as follows:

```
model.fit(train_x, train_y, epochs=50)
```

model.evaluate()

The model.evaluate() function returns the loss value and metrics values for the model using test dataset. What it returns and the accepted arguments are similar to the model.fit() function, but it does not train the model any further.

```
model.evaluate(test_x, test_y)
```

model.predict()

`model.predict()` is the function we use to make single predictions. While the `model.evaluate()` function requires labels, the `model.predict()` function does not require labels. It just makes predictions using the trained model, as shown here:

```
model.evaluate(sample_x)
```

Custom Training

Instead of following standard training options which allows you to use functions such as `model.compile()`, `model.fit()`, `model.evaluate()`, and `model.predict()`, you can fully customize this process.

To be able to define a custom training loop, you have to use a `tf.GradientTape()`. `tf.GradientTape()` records operations for automatic differentiation, which is very useful for implementing machine learning algorithms such as backpropagation during training. In other words, `tf.GradientTape()` allows us to track TensorFlow computations and calculate gradients.

For custom training, we follow these steps:

- Set optimizer, loss function, and metrics.

- Run a for loop for the number of epochs.

    - Run a nested loop for each batch of each epoch:

    - Work with `tf.GradientTape()` to calculate and record loss and to conduct backpropagation.

    - Run the optimizer.

    - Calculate, record, and print out metric results.

The following lines show an example of the standard method for training. Just in two lines, you can configure and train your model.

```
model.compile(optimizer=Adam(), loss=SCC(from_logits=True),
metrics=[SCA()])
model.fit(x_train, y_train, epochs=epochs)
```

The following lines, on the other hand, show how you can achieve the same results with a custom training loop.

```
# Instantiate optimizer, loss, and metric
optimizer, loss_fn, accuracy = Adam(), SCC(from_logits=True),
SCA()
# Convert NumPy to TF Dataset object
train_dataset = (Dataset.from_tensor_slices((x_train, y_
train)).shuffle(buffer_size=1024).batch(batch_size=64))

for epoch in range(epochs):
    # Iterate over the batches of the dataset.
    for step, (x_batch_train, y_batch_train) in
    enumerate(train_dataset):
        # Open a GradientTape to record the operations, which
        enables auto-differentiation.
        with tf.GradientTape() as tape:
            # The operations that the layer applies to its
            inputs are going to be recorded
            logits = model(x_batch_train, training=True)
            loss_value = loss_fn(y_batch_train, logits)
        # Use the tape to automatically retrieve the gradients
        of the trainable variables
        grads = tape.gradient(loss_value, model.trainable_weights)
        # Run one step of gradient descent by updating
        # the value of the variables to minimize the loss.
```

```
    optimizer.apply_gradients(zip(grads, model.trainable_
    weights))
  # Metrics related part
    accuracy.update_state(y_batch_train, logits)
    if step % int(len(train_dataset)/5) == 0: #Print out
      print(step, "/", len(train_dataset)," | ",end="")
  print("\rFor Epoch %.0f, Accuracy: %.4f" % (epoch+1,
  float(accuracy.result()),))
  accuracy.reset_states()
```

As you can see, it is much more complicated, and therefore, you should only use custom training when it is absolutely necessary. You may also customize the individual training step, model.evaluate() function, and even model.predict() function. Therefore, TensorFlow almost always provide enough flexibility for researchers and custom model developers. In this book, we take advantage of custom training in Chapter 12.

Saving and Loading the Model

We just learned how to build a neural network, and this information will be crucial for the case studies in the upcoming chapters. But we also would like to use the models we trained in real-world applications. Therefore, we need to save our model so that it can be reused.

We can save an entire model to a single artifact. When we saved the entire model, it contains

- The model's architecture and configuration data

- The model's optimized weights

- The model's compilation information (model. compile() info)

- The optimizer and its latest state

TensorFlow provides two formats to save models:

- TensorFlow SavedModel Format

- Keras HDF5 (or H5) Format

Although the old HDF5 format was quite popular previously, SavedModel has become the recommended format to save models in TensorFlow. The key difference between HDF5 and SavedModel is that HDF5 uses object configs to save the model architecture, while SavedModel saves the execution graph. The practical consequence of this difference is significant. SavedModels can save custom objects such as models that are built with Model Subclassing or custom-built layers without the original code. To be able to save the custom objects in HDF5 format, there are extra steps involved, which makes HDF5 less appealing.

Saving the Model

Saving the model in one of these formats is very easy. The desired format can be selected with an argument (save_format) passed in the model. save() function.

To save a model in the SavedModel format, we can use the following line:

```
model.save("My_SavedModel")
```

If you'd like to save your model in the HDF5 format, we can simply use the same function with the save_format argument:

```
model.save("My_H5Model", save_format="h5")
```

For the HDF5 format, you can alternatively use Keras's save_model() function, as shown here:

```
tf.keras.models.save_model("My_H5Model")
```

After saving the model, the files containing the model can be found in your temporary Google Colab directory.

Loading the Model

After you saved the model files, you can easily load and reconstruct the model you saved before. To load our model, we make use of the load_ model() function offered by Keras API. The following lines can be used to load a model saved in either format:

```
import tensorflow as tf
reconstructed_model = tf.keras.models.load_model
( 'My_SavedModel' )
```

You can use the loaded model just like you use a model you trained. The following lines are the exact copy of the model.evaluate() function used for the freshly trained model:

```
test_loss, test_acc = reconstructed_model.evaluate
( x_test,  y_test, verbose=2)
print('\nTest accuracy:', test_acc)
```

Conclusion

Now that we covered how we can use TensorFlow for our deep learning pipeline along with some TensorFlow basics, we can start covering different types of neural network concepts along with their corresponding case studies. Our first neural network type is feedforward neural networks or, in other words, multilayer perceptron.

120

CHAPTER 6

Feedforward Neural Networks

In this chapter, we will cover the most generic version of neural networks, feedforward neural networks. Feedforward neural networks are a group of artificial neural networks in which the connections between neurons do not form a cycle. Connections between neurons are unidirectional and move in only forward direction from input layer through hidden layers and to output later. In other words, the reason these networks are called feedforward is that the flow of information takes place in the forward direction.

Recurrent Neural Networks, which we will cover in Chapter 8, are improved versions of feedforward neural networks in which bidirectionality is added. Therefore, they are not considered feedforward anymore.

Feedforward neural networks are mainly used for supervised learning tasks. They are especially useful in analytical applications and quantitative studies where traditional machine learning algorithms are also used.

Feedforward neural networks are very easy to build, but they are not scalable in computer vision and natural language processing (NLP) problems. Also, feedforward neural networks do not have a memory

© Orhan Gazi Yalçın 2021
O. G. Yalçın, *Applied Neural Networks with TensorFlow 2*,
https://doi.org/10.1007/978-1-4842-6513-0_6

structure which is useful in sequence data. To address the scalability and memory issues, alternative artificial neural networks such as convolutional neural networks and recurrent neural networks are developed, which will be covered in the next chapters.

You may run into different names for feedforward neural networks such as artificial neural networks, regular neural networks, regular nets, multilayer perceptron, and some others. There is unfortunately an ambiguity, but in this book, we always use the term feedforward neural network.

Deep and Shallow Feedforward Neural Networks

Every feedforward neural network must have two layers: (i) an input layer and (ii) an output layer. The main goal of a feedforward neural network is to approximate a function using (i) the input values fed from the input layer and (ii) the final output values in the output layer by comparing them with the label values.

Shallow Feedforward Neural Network

When a model only has an input and an output layer for function approximation, it is considered as a shallow feedforward neural network. It is also referred to as single-layer perceptron, shown in Figure 6-1.

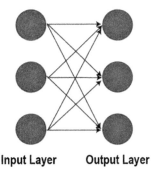

Input Layer   **Output Layer**

Figure 6-1. *Shallow Feedforward Neural Network or Single-Layer Perceptron*

The output values in a shallow feedforward neural network are computed directly from the sum of the product of its weights with the corresponding input values and some bias. Shallow feedforward neural networks are not useful to approximate nonlinear functions. To address this issue, we embed hidden layers between input and output layers.

Deep Feedforward Neural Network

When a feedforward neural network has one or more hidden layers which enable it to approximate more complex function, this model is considered as a deep feedforward neural network. It is also referred to as multilayer perceptron, shown in Figure 6-2.

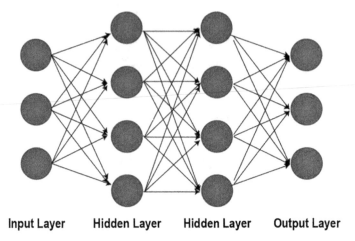

Input Layer   Hidden Layer   Hidden Layer   Output Layer

Figure 6-2. *Deep Feedforward Neural Network or Multilayer Perceptron*

Every neuron in a layer is connected to the neurons in the next layer and utilizes an activation function.

Universal Approximation Theory indicates that a feedforward neural network can approximate any real-valued continuous functions on compact subsets of Euclidean space. The theory also implies that when given appropriate weights, neural networks can represent all the potential functions.

Since deep feedforward neural networks can approximate any linear or nonlinear function, they are widely used in real-world applications, both for classification and regression problems. In the case study of this chapter, we also build a deep feedforward neural network to have acceptable results.

Feedforward Neural Network Architecture

In a feedforward neural network, the leftmost layer is called the input layer, consisting of input neurons. The rightmost layer is called the output layer, consisting of a set of output neurons or a single output neuron. The layers in the middle are called hidden layers with several neurons ensuring nonlinear approximation.

In a feedforward neural network, we take advantage of an optimizer with backpropagation, activation functions, and cost functions as well as additional bias on top of weights. These terms are already explained in Chapter 3 and, therefore, omitted here. Please refer to Chapter 3 for more detail. Let's take a deeper look at the layers of feedforward neural networks.

Layers in a Feedforward Neural Network

As mentioned earlier, our generic feedforward neural network architecture consists of three types of layers:

- An input layer

- An output layer

- A number of hidden layers

Input Layer

Input layer is the very first layer of feedforward neural network, which is used to feed data into the network. Input layer does not utilize an activation function and its sole purpose to get the data into the system. The number of neurons in an input layer must be equal to the number of features (i.e., explanatory variables) fed into the system. For instance, if we are using five different explanatory variables to predict one response variable, our model's input layer must have five neurons.

Output Layer

Output layer is the very last layer of the feedforward neural network, which is used to output the prediction. The number of neurons in the output layer is decided based on the nature of the problem. For regression problems, we aim to predict a single value, and therefore, we set a single neuron in our output layer. For classification problems, the number of neurons is equal to the number of classes. For example, for binary classification, we need two neurons in the output layer, whereas for multi-class classification with five different classes, we need five neurons in the output layer. Output layers also take advantage of an activation function depending on the nature of the problem (e.g., a linear activation for regression and softmax for classification problems).

Hidden Layer

Hidden layers are created to ensure the approximation of the nonlinear functions. We can add as many hidden layers as we desire, and the number of neurons at each layer can be changed. Therefore, as opposed to input and output layers, we are much more flexible with hidden layers. Hidden layers are appropriate layers to introduce bias terms, which are not neurons, but constants added to the calculations that affect each neuron in the next layer. Hidden layers also take advantage of activation functions such as Sigmoid, Tanh, and ReLU.

In the next section, we will build a deep feedforward neural network to show all these layers in action. Thanks to Keras Sequential API, the process will be very easy.

Case Study | Fuel Economics with Auto MPG

Now that we covered the basics of feedforward neural networks, we can build a deep feedforward neural network to predict how many miles can a car travel with one gallon of gas. This term is usually referred to as miles per gallon (MPG). For this case study, we use one of the classic datasets: Auto MPG dataset. Auto MPG was initially used in the 1983 American Statistical Association Exposition. The data concerns prediction of city-cycle fuel consumption in miles per gallon in terms of three multivalued discrete and five continuous attributes. For this case study, we benefit from a tutorial written by François Chollet, the creator of Keras library.[1]

Let's dive into the code. Please create a new Colab Notebook via `https://colab.research.google.com`.

Initial Installs and Imports

We will take advantage of the TensorFlow Docs library which is not included in the Google Colab Notebook initially. So, we start the case study with a library installation with the following code:

```
# Install tensorflow_docs
```

---

[1]Copyright (c) 2017 François Chollet

Permission is hereby granted, free of charge, to any person obtaining a copy of this software and associated documentation files (the "Software"), to deal in the Software without restriction, including without limitation the rights to use, copy, modify, merge, publish, distribute, sublicense, and/or sell copies of the Software, and to permit persons to whom the Software is furnished to do so, subject to the following conditions:

The above copyright notice and this permission notice shall be included in all copies or substantial portions of the Software.

THE SOFTWARE IS PROVIDED "AS IS", WITHOUT WARRANTY OF ANY KIND, EXPRESS OR IMPLIED, INCLUDING BUT NOT LIMITED TO THE WARRANTIES OF MERCHANTABILITY, FITNESS FOR A PARTICULAR PURPOSE AND NONINFRINGEMENT. IN NO EVENT SHALL THE AUTHORS OR COPYRIGHT HOLDERS BE LIABLE FOR ANY CLAIM, DAMAGES OR OTHER LIABILITY, WHETHER IN AN ACTION OF CONTRACT, TORT OR OTHERWISE, ARISING FROM, OUT OF OR IN CONNECTION WITH THE SOFTWARE OR THE USE OR OTHER DEALINGS IN THE SOFTWARE.

```
!pip install -q git+https://github.com/tensorflow/docs
```

There are a number of libraries we will utilize in this case study. Let's import the ones we will use in the beginning:

```
# Import the initial libraries to be used
import tensorflow as tf
import pandas as pd
import numpy as np
import matplotlib.pyplot as plt
```

Please note that there will be some other imports, which will be shared in their corresponding sections.

Downloading the Auto MPG Data

Even though Auto MPG is a very popular dataset, we still cannot access the dataset via TensorFlow's dataset module. However, there is a very straightforward way (thanks to the get_file() function of tf.keras. utils module) to load external data into our Google Colab Notebook with the following lines of code:

```
autompg = tf.keras.utils.get_file(
        fname='auto-mpg', #filename for local directory
        origin='http://archive.ics.uci.edu/ml/machine-learning-
databases/auto-mpg/auto-mpg.data',#URL address to retrieve the
dataset
```

Note that we retrieve the dataset from UCI Machine Learning Repository. UC Irvine provides an essential repository, along with Kaggle, in which you can access to a vast number of popular datasets.

Data Preparation

When we look at the UC Irvine's Auto MPG page, we can see a list of attributes which represents all the variables in the Auto MPG dataset, which is shared here:

Attribute Information:

- **mpg**: Continuous (response variable)

- **cylinders**: Multivalued discrete

- **displacement**: Continuous

- **horsepower**: Continuous

- **weight**: Continuous

- **acceleration**: Continuous

- **model year**: Multivalued discrete

- **origin**: Multivalued discrete

- **car name**: String (unique for each instance)

DataFrame Creation

As a best practice, we will name our dataset columns with these attribute names and import from our Google Colab directory since we already saved it in the previous section:

```
column_names = ['mpg', 'cylinders', 'displacement', 'HP',
'weight', 'acceleration', 'modelyear', 'origin']
df = pd.read_csv(autompg, # name of the csv file
        sep=" ", # separator in the csv file
        comment='\t', #remove car name sep. with '\t'
        names=column_names,
        na_values = '?', #NA values are coded as '?'
```

```
        skipinitialspace=True)
df.head(2) #list the first two row of the dataset
```

Here is the result of df.head(2), shown in Figure 6-3.

	mpg	cylinders	displacement	HP	weight	acceleration	modelyear	origin
0	18.0	8	307.0	130.0	3504.0	12.0	70	1
1	15.0	8	350.0	165.0	3693.0	11.5	70	1

Figure 6-3. *The First Two Lines of the Auto MPG Dataset*

Dropping Null Values

We can check the number of null values with the following code:

```
df.isna().sum()
```

The output we get is shown in Figure 6-4.

```
 mpg             0
 cylinders       0
 displacement    0
 HP              6
 weight          0
 acceleration    0
 modelyear       0
 origin          0
 dtype: int64
```

Figure 6-4. *Null Value Counts in the Auto MPG Dataset*

We have six null values in the HP column. There are several ways to deal with the null values. Firstly, we can drop them. Secondly, we can fill them using a method such as (a) filling with the mean value of other observations or (b) use a regression method to interpolate their value. For the sake of simplicity, we will drop them with the following code:

```
df = df.dropna() # Drop null values
df = df.reset_index(drop=True) # Reset index to tidy up the
dataset
df.show()
```

Handling Categorical Variables

Let's review our dataset with the info attribute of Pandas DataFrame object:

```
df.info() # Get an overview of the dataset
```

As shown in Figure 6-5, We can see that Auto MPG dataset has 392 car observations with no null values. The variables *cylinders*, *modelyear*, and *origin* are the categorical variables we should consider using dummy variables.

```
<class 'pandas.core.frame.DataFrame'>
RangeIndex: 392 entries, 0 to 391
Data columns (total 8 columns):
 #   Column        Non-Null Count   Dtype
---  ------        --------------   -----
 0   mpg           392 non-null     float64
 1   cylinders     392 non-null     int64
 2   displacement  392 non-null     float64
 3   HP            392 non-null     float64
 4   weight        392 non-null     float64
 5   acceleration  392 non-null     float64
 6   modelyear     392 non-null     int64
 7   origin        392 non-null     int64
dtypes: float64(5), int64(3)
memory usage: 24.6 KB
```

Figure 6-5. *Overview of the Auto MPG Dataset*

Dummy Variable is a special variable type that takes only the value 0 or 1 to indicate the absence or presence of a categorical effect. In machine learning studies, every category of a categorical variable is encoded as a dummy variable. But, omitting one of these categories as a dummy variable is a good practice, which prevents multicollinearity problem.

Using dummy variables is especially important if the values of a categorical variable do not indicate a mathematical relationship. This is absolutely valid for origin variable since the values 1, 2, and 3 represent the United States, Europe, and Japan. Therefore, we need to generate dummies for *origin* variable, drop the first one to prevent multicollinearity, and drop the initial *origin* variable (origin variable is now represented with the generated dummy variables). We can achieve these tasks with the following lines of code:

```
def one_hot_origin_encoder(df):
        df_copy = df.copy()
        df_copy['EU']=df_copy['origin'].map({1:0,2:1,3:0})
        df_copy['Japan']=df_copy['origin'].map({1:0,2:0,3:1})
        df_copy = df_copy.drop('origin',axis=1)
        return df_copy
df_clean = one_hot_origin_encoder(df)
```

Here is the result of df_clean.head(2), shown in Figure 6-6.

	mpg	cylinders	displacement	HP	weight	acceleration	modelyear	EU	Japan
0	18.0	8	307.0	130.0	3504.0	12.0	70	0	0
1	15.0	8	350.0	165.0	3693.0	11.5	70	0	0

Figure 6-6. *The First Two Lines of the Auto MPG Dataset with Dummy Variables*

Splitting Auto MPG for Training and Testing

Now that we cleaned our dataset, it is time to split them into train and test sets. Train set is used to train our neural network (i.e., optimize the neuron weights) to minimize the errors. Test set is used as the never-been-seen observations to test the performance of our trained neural network.

Since our dataset is in the form of a Pandas DataFrame object, we can use sample attribute. We keep the 80% of the observations for training and 20% for testing. Additionally, we also split the label from the features so that we can feed the features as input. Then, check the results with labels.

These tasks can be achieved with the following lines of codes:

```
# Training Dataset and X&Y Split
# Test Dataset and X&Y Split
# For Training
train = df_clean.sample(frac=0.8,random_state=0)
train_x = train.drop('mpg',axis=1)
train_y = train['mpg']
# For Testing
test = df_clean.drop(train.index)
test_x = test.drop('mpg',axis=1)
test_y = test['mpg']
```

Now that we split our dataset into train and test sets, it is time to normalize our data. As mentioned in Chapter 3, feature scaling is an important part of the data preparation. Without feature scaling, a feature can adversely affect our model.

We need to extract the means and standard deviations to manually apply normalization to our data. We can generate this dataset with ease, using the following code:

```
train_stats = train_x.describe().transpose()
```

You can obtain the following output in Figure 6-7 by running train_stats.

	count	mean	std	min	25%	50%	75%	max
cylinders	314.0	5.477707	1.699788	3.0	4.00	4.0	8.00	8.0
displacement	314.0	195.318471	104.331589	68.0	105.50	151.0	265.75	455.0
HP	314.0	104.869427	38.096214	46.0	76.25	94.5	128.00	225.0
weight	314.0	2990.251592	843.898596	1649.0	2256.50	2822.5	3608.00	5140.0
acceleration	314.0	15.559236	2.789230	8.0	13.80	15.5	17.20	24.8
modelyear	314.0	75.898089	3.675642	70.0	73.00	76.0	79.00	82.0
EU	314.0	0.178344	0.383413	0.0	0.00	0.0	0.00	1.0
Japan	314.0	0.197452	0.398712	0.0	0.00	0.0	0.00	1.0

Figure 6-7. *train_stats DataFrame for Train Set Statistics*

Now that we have the mean and standard deviation values for training set features, it is time to normalize the train and test sets. The custom **normalizer(x)** function can be used for train, test, and new observation sets.

```
# Feature scaling with the mean
# and std. dev. values in train_stats
def normalizer(x):
  return (x-train_stats['mean'])/train_stats['std']
train_x_scaled = normalizer(train_x)
test_x_scaled = normalizer(test_x)
```

Note that we do not normalize the label (y) values since their wide range doesn't pose a threat for our model.

Model Building and Training

Now, our data is cleaned and prepared for our feedforward neural network pipeline. Let's build our model and train it.

Tensorflow Imports

We already had some initial imports. In this part, we will import the remaining modules and libraries to build, train, and evaluate our feedforward neural network.

Remaining imports consist of the following libraries:

```
# Importing the required Keras modules containing model and
layers
from tensorflow.keras.models import Sequential
from tensorflow.keras.layers import Dense
# TensorFlow Docs Imports for Evaluation
import tensorflow_docs as tfdocs
import tensorflow_docs.plots
import tensorflow_docs.modeling
```

Sequential() is our API for model building, whereas Dense() is the layer we will use in our feedforward neural network. tf.docs module will be used for model evaluation.

Model with Sequential API

After creating a model object with Sequential API and naming it model, we can shape our empty model by adding Dense() layers. Each dense layer – except the last one – requires an activation function. We will use ReLU for this case study, but feel free to set other activation functions such as Tanh or Sigmoid. Our input_shape parameter must be equal to the number of features, and our output layer must have only one neuron since this is a regression case.

```
# Creating a Sequential Model and adding the layers
model = Sequential()
model.add(Dense(8,activation=tf.nn.relu, input_shape= [train_x.
shape[1]])),
```

```
model.add(Dense(32,activation=tf.nn.relu)),
model.add(Dense(16,activation=tf.nn.relu)),
model.add(Dense(1))
```

We can see the flowchart of model with a single line of code; see Figure 6-8:

```
tf.keras.utils.plot_model(model, show_shapes=True)
```

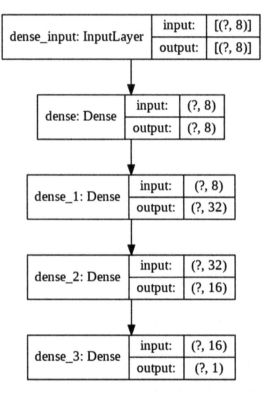

Figure 6-8. *The Flowchart of the Feedforward Neural Network for Auto MPG*

Model Configuration

Now that we build the main network structure of our neural network, we need to configure our optimizer, cost function, and metrics before initiating the training. We will use Adam optimizer and mean squared error (MSE) in our neural network. Additionally, TensorFlow will provide us mean absolute error (MAE) values as well as MSE values. We can configure our model with the following code:

```
# Optimizer, Cost, and Metric Configuration
model.compile(optimizer='adam',
              loss='mse',
              metrics=['mse','mae']
)
```

As mentioned in Chapter 3, one of the powerful methods to fight overfitting is early stopping. With the following lines of code, we will set an early stopper if we do not see a valuable improvement for 50 epochs.

```
# Early Stop Configuration
early_stop=tf.keras.callbacks.EarlyStopping( monitor=
'val_loss', patience=50)
```

Now that we configured our model, we can train our model with the fit attribute of our model object:

```
# Fitting the Model and Saving the Callback Histories
history=model.fit(
        x=train_x_scaled,
        y=train_y,
        epochs=1000,
        validation_split = 0.2,
```

```
    verbose=0,
    callbacks=[early_stop,
          tfdocs.modeling.EpochDots()
          ])
```

We set aside 20% of our train set for validation. Therefore, our neural network will evaluate the model even before the test set. We set the epoch value to 1000, but it will stop early if it cannot observe a valuable improvement on the validation loss/cost. Finally, callbacks parameter will save valuable information for us to evaluate our model with plots and other useful tools.

Evaluating the Results

Now that we trained our model, we can evaluate the results. Our **TensorFlow Docs** library allows us to plot the loss values at each epoch. We can create a new object using HistoryPlotter to create the object with following code:

```
plot_obj=tfdocs.plots.HistoryPlotter(smoothing_std=2)
```

After creating the object, we can use the plot attribute to create the plot, and we can set the ylim and ylabel values just as in Matplotlib with the following code:

```
plot_obj.plot({'Auto MPG': history}, metric = "mae")
plt.ylim([0, 10])
plt.ylabel('MAE [mpg]')
```

Figure 6-9 shows the overview of our loss values at each epoch.

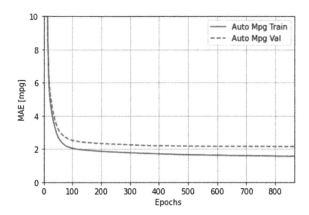

Figure 6-9. *The Line Plot Showing Mean Absolute Error Values at Each Epoch*

With the evaluate attribute of the model, we can also evaluate our model using test set. The following lines will generate loss, MAE, and MSE values using our test set as shown in Figure 6-10:

```
loss,mae,mse=model.evaluate(test_x_scaled,
                            test_y,
                            verbose=2)
print("Testing set Mean Abs Error: {:5.2f} MPG".format(mae))
```

```
3/3 - 0s - loss: 6.2608 - mse: 6.2608 - mae: 1.9632
Testing set Mean Abs Error:  6.26 MPG
```

Figure 6-10. *Evaluation Results for the Trained Model for Auto MPG*

We can generate predictions using the test set labels with a single line of code:

```
test_preds = model.predict(test_x_scaled).flatten()
```

Finally, we can plot the test set labels (actual values) against the predictions generated with the test set features (see Figure 6-11) with the following lines of code:

```
evaluation_plot = plt.axes(aspect='equal')
plt.scatter(test_y, test_preds)#Scatter Plot
plt.ylabel('Predictions [mpg]')#Y for Predictions
plt.xlabel('Actual Values [mpg]')#X for Actual Values
plt.xlim([0, 50])
plt.ylim([0, 50])
plt.plot([0, 50], [0, 50]) #line plot for comparison
```

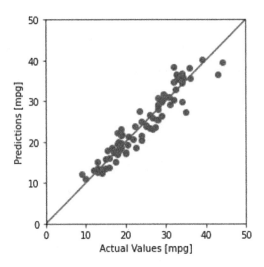

Figure 6-11. *The Scatter Plot for Actual Test Labels vs. Their Prediction Values*

We can also generate a histogram showing the distribution of error terms around zero (see Figure 6-12), which is an important indication of bias in our model. The following lines of code generate the said histogram:

```
error = test_preds - test_y
plt.hist(error, bins = 25)
plt.xlabel("Prediction Error [mpg]")
plt.ylabel("Count")
```

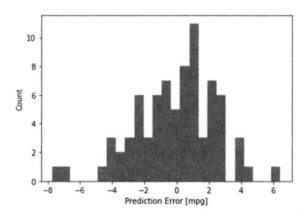

Figure 6-12. *The Histogram Showing the Error Distribution of the Model Around Zero*

Making Predictions with a New Observation

Both the scatter plot and the histogram we generated earlier show that our model is healthy, and our loss values are also in an acceptable range. Therefore, we can use our trained model to make new predictions, using our own dummy observation.

I will create a dummy car with the following lines of code:

```
# Prediction for Single Observation
# What is the MPG of a car with the following info:
new_car = pd.DataFrame([[8,    #cylinders
                        307.0, #displacement
                        130.0, #HP
                        5504.0, #weight
                        12.0, #acceleration
```

141

```
            70, #modelyear
            1 #origin
    ]], columns=column_names[1:])
```

This code will create the following Pandas DataFrame with single observation, shown in Figure 6-13.

	cylinders	displacement	HP	weight	acceleration	modelyear	origin
0	8	307.0	130.0	5504.0	12.0	70	1

Figure 6-13. *A Pandas DataFrame with Single Observation*

We need to create dummy variables and normalize the observation before feeding into the trained model. After these operations, we can simply use the predict attribute of our model. We can complete these operations with these lines:

```
new_car = normalizer(one_hot_origin_encoder(new_car))
new_car_mpg = model.predict(new_car).flatten()
print('The predicted miles per gallon value for this car is:',
new_car_mpg)
```

The preceding code gives this output:

```
The prediction miles per gallon value for this car is:
[14.727904]
```

Conclusion

Feedforward neural networks are artificial neural networks that are widely used in analytical applications and quantitative studies. They are the oldest artificial neural networks and often named as multilayer perceptron. They are considered as the backbone of the artificial neural network family. You can find them embedded at the end of a convolutional neural network. Recurrent neural networks are developed from feedforward neural networks, with added bidirectionality.

In the next chapter, we will dive into convolutional neural networks, a group of neural network family which are widely used in computer vision, image and video processing, and many alike.

CHAPTER 7

Convolutional Neural Networks

It is safe to say that one of the most powerful supervised deep learning models is convolutional neural networks (abbreviated as CNN or ConvNet). CNN is a class of deep learning networks, mostly applied to image data. However, CNN structures can be used in a variety of real-world problems including, *but not limited to*, image recognition, natural language processing, video analysis, anomaly detection, drug discovery, health risk assessment, recommender systems, and time-series forecasting.

CNNs achieve a high level of accuracy by assembling complex patterns using the more basic patterns found in the training data. For instance, from lines to an eyebrow, from two eyebrows to a human face, and then to a full human figure, CNNs can correctly detect humans in an image by using mere lines. To assemble these patterns, CNNs require a small amount of data preparation since their algorithm automatically performs these operations. This characteristic of CNNs offers an advantage compared to the other models used for image processing.

© Orhan Gazi Yalçın 2021
O. G. Yalçın, *Applied Neural Networks with TensorFlow 2*,
https://doi.org/10.1007/978-1-4842-6513-0_7

Today, the overall architecture of the CNNs is already streamlined. The final part of CNNs is very similar to feedforward neural networks (RegularNets, multilayer perceptron), where there are fully connected layers of neurons with weights and biases. Just like in feedforward neural networks, there is a loss function (e.g., crossentropy, MSE), a number of activation functions, and an optimizer (e.g., SGD, Adam optimizer) in CNNs. Additionally, though, in CNNs, there are also Convolutional layers, Pooling layers, and Flatten layers.

In the next section, we will take a look at why using CNN for image processing is such a good idea.

Note   I will usually refer to image data to exemplify the CNN concepts. But, please note that these examples are still relevant for different types of data such as audio waves or stock prices.

Why Convolutional Neural Networks?

The main architectural characteristic of feedforward neural networks is the intralayer connectedness of all the neurons. For example, when we have grayscale images with 28 x 28 pixels, we end up having 784 (28 x 28 x 1) neurons in a layer that seems manageable. However, most images have way more pixels, and they are not in grayscale. Therefore, when we have a set of color images in 4K ultra HD, we end up with 26,542,080 (4096 x 2160 x 3) different neurons in the input layer that are connected to the neurons in the next layer, which is not manageable. Therefore, we can say that feedforward neural networks are not scalable for image classification. However, especially when it comes to images, there seems to be little correlation or relation between two individual pixels unless they are close to each other. This important discovery led to the idea of Convolutional layers and Pooling layers found in every CNN architecture.

CNN Architecture

Usually, in a CNN architecture, there are several convolutional layers and pooling layers at the beginning, which are mainly used to simplify the image data complexity and reduce their sizes. In addition, they are very useful to extract complex patterns from the basic patterns observed in images. After using several convolutional and pooling layers (supported with activation functions), we reshape our data from two-dimensional or three-dimensional arrays into a one-dimensional array with a Flatten layer. After the flatten layer, a set of fully connected layers take the flattened one-dimensional array as input and complete the classification or regression task. Let's take a look at these layers individually.

Layers in a CNN

We are capable of using many different layers in a convolutional neural network. However, convolutional, pooling, and fully connected layers are the most important ones. Therefore, let's quickly cover these layers before we implement them in our case studies.

Convolutional Layers

A convolutional layer is the very first layer where we extract features from the images in our datasets. Since pixels are only related to the adjacent and other close pixels, convolution allows us to preserve the relationship between different parts of an image. The task of a convolutional layer merely is filtering the image with a smaller pixel filter to decrease the size of the image without losing the relationship between pixels. When we apply convolution to a 5 x 5 pixel image by using a 3 x 3 pixel filter with a 1 x 1 stride (1-pixel shift at each step), we end up having a 3 x 3 pixel output (64% decrease in complexity) as shown in Figure 7-1.

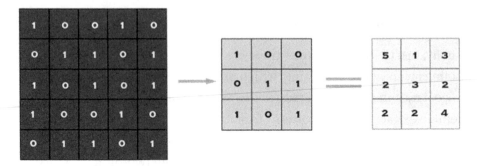

Figure 7-1. *Convolution of 5 x 5 Pixel Image with 3 x 3 Pixel Filter (Stride = 1 x 1 pixel)*

Filtering

Filtering is performed by multiplying each value in a part of the image data with the corresponding filter value. In Figure 7-2, the very first operation is as follows. (Please refer to Table 7-1 for all convolution operations shown in Figure 7-1).

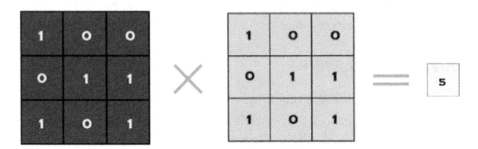

Figure 7-2. *The Very First Filtering Operation for the Convolution Shown in Figure 7-1*

Table 7-1. *The Table of Calculations for Figure 7-2*

Rows	Calculations	Result
1st row	(1x0) + (0x0) + (0x0) +	
2nd row	(0x0) + (1x1) + (1x1) +	= 5
3rd row	(1x1) + (0x0) + (1x1)	

Using a too large filter would reduce the complexity more, but also cause the loss of important patterns. Therefore, we should set an optimal filter size to keep the patterns and adequately reduce the complexity of our data.

Strides

Stride is a parameter to set how many pixels will the filter shift after each operation. For the example earlier

- If we select a 1 x 1 pixel stride, we end up shifting the filter 9 times to process all the data.

- If we select a 2 x 2 pixel stride, we can process the entire 5 x 5 pixel image in 4 filter operations.

Using a large stride value would decrease the number of filter calculations. A large stride value would significantly reduce the complexity of the model, yet we might lose some of the patterns along the process. Therefore, we should always set an optimal stride value – not too large, not too small.

Pooling Layer

When constructing CNNs, it is almost standard practice to insert pooling layers after each convolutional layer to reduce the spatial size of the representation to reduce the parameter counts, which reduces the computational complexity. In addition, pooling layers also help with the overfitting problem.

For pooling operation, we select a pooling size to reduce the amount of the parameters by selecting the maximum, average, or sum values inside these pixels. Max pooling, one of the most common pooling techniques, may be demonstrated as follows.

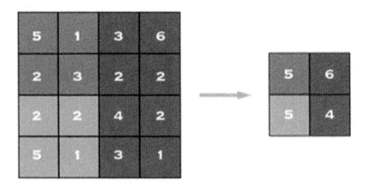

Figure 7-3. *Max Pooling by 2 x 2*

In pooling layers, after setting a pooling size of N x N pixels, we divide the image data into N x N pixel portions to choose the maximum, average, or sum value of these divided portions.

For the example in Figure 7-3, we split our 4 x 4 pixel image into 2 x 2 pixel portions, which gives us 4 portions in total. Since we are using max pooling, we select the maximum value inside these portions and create a reduced image that still contains the patterns in the original image data.

Selecting an optimal value for N x N is also crucial to keep the patterns in the data while achieving an adequate level of complexity reduction.

A Set of Fully Connected Layers

Fully connected network in a CNN is an embedded feedforward neural network, where each neuron in a layer is linked to the neurons in the next layer to determine the true relation and effect of each parameter on the labels. Since our time-space complexity is vastly reduced thanks to convolution and pooling layers, we can construct a fully connected network at the end of our CNN to classify our images. A set of fully connected layers looks like as shown in Figure 7-4:

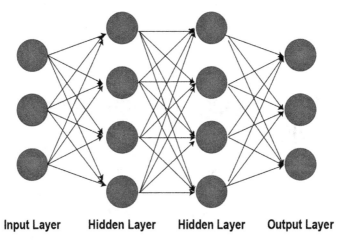

Input Layer   Hidden Layer   Hidden Layer   Output Layer

Figure 7-4. *A Fully Connected Layer with Two Hidden Layers*

A Full CNN Model

Now that you have some idea about the individual layers of CNNs, it is time to share an overview look of a complete convolutional neural network in Figure 7-5:

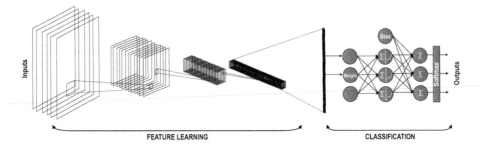

Figure 7-5. *A Convolutional Neural Network Example*

While the feature learning phase is performed with the help of convolution and pooling layers, classification is performed with the set of fully connected layers.

Case Study | Image Classification with MNIST

Now that we covered the basics of convolutional neural networks, we can build a CNN for image classification. For this case study, we use the most cliché dataset used for image classification: MNIST dataset, which stands for Modified National Institute of Standards and Technology database. It is an extensive database of handwritten digits that is commonly used for training various image processing systems.

Downloading the MNIST Data

The MNIST dataset is one of the most common datasets used for image classification and accessible from many different sources. Tensorflow allows us to import and download the MNIST dataset directly from its API. Therefore, we start with the following two lines to import TensorFlow and MNIST dataset under the Keras API.

```
import tensorflow as tf
import tensorflow_datasets as tfds
(x_train,y_train),(x_test,y_test)=tfds.as_numpy(tfds.
load('mnist', #name of the dataset
        split=['train', 'test'], #both train & test sets
        batch_size=-1, #all data in single batch
        as_supervised=True, #only input and label
        shuffle_files=True #shuffle data to randomize
  ))
```

The MNIST database contains 60,000 training images and 10,000 testing images taken from American Census Bureau employees and American high school students. Therefore, in the second line, we separate these two groups as train and test and also separate the labels and the images. x_train and x_test parts contain grayscale RGB codes (from 0 to 255), while y_train and y_test parts contain labels from 0 to 9, which represents which number they actually are. To visualize these numbers, we can get help from Matplotlib.

```
import matplotlib.pyplot as plt
img_index = 7777 #You may pick a number up to 60,000
print("The digit in the image:", y_train[img_index])
plt.imshow(x_train[img_index].reshape(28,28),cmap='Greys')
```

When we run the preceding code, we will get the grayscale visualization of the image as shown in Figure 7-6.

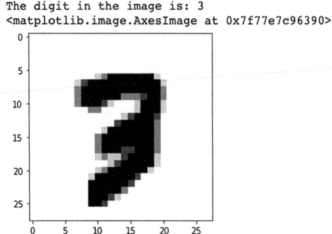

The digit in the image is: 3
<matplotlib.image.AxesImage at 0x7f77e7c96390>

Figure 7-6. *A Visualization of the Sample Image and Its Label*

We also need to know the shape of the dataset to channel it to the convolutional neural network. Therefore, we use the shape attribute of the NumPy array with the following code:

```
x_train.shape
```

The output we get is (60000, 28, 28, 1). As you might have guessed, 60000 represents the number of images in the training dataset; (28, 28) represents the size of the image, 28 x 28 pixels; and 1 shows that our images are not colored.

Reshaping and Normalizing the Images

With TensorFlow's dataset API, we already created a four-dimensional NumPy array for training, which is the required array dimension. On the other hand, we must normalize our data as it is a best practice in neural network models. We can achieve this by dividing the grayscale RGB codes to 255 (which is the maximum grayscale RGB code minus the minimum grayscale RGB code). This can be done with the following code:

```
# Making sure that the values are float so that we can get
decimal points after division
x_train = x_train.astype('float32')
x_test = x_test.astype('float32')
# Normalizing the grayscale RGB codes by dividing it to the
"max minus min grayscale RGB value".
x_train /= 255
x_test /= 255
print('x_train shape:', x_train.shape)
print('Number of images in x_train', x_train.shape[0])
print('Number of images in x_test', x_test.shape[0])
```

Building the Convolutional Neural Network

We build our model by using high-level Keras Sequential API to simplify
the development process. I would like to mention that there are other
high-level TensorFlow APIs such as Estimators, Keras Functional API,
and another Keras Sequential API method, which helps us create neural
networks with high-level knowledge. These different options may lead to
confusion since they all vary in their implementation structure. Therefore,
if you see entirely different codes for the same neural network, although
they all use TensorFlow, this is why.

We use the most straightforward TensorFlow API – Keras Sequential
API – since we don't need much flexibility. Therefore, we import the
Sequential model object from Keras and add Conv2D, MaxPooling,
Flatten, Dropout, and Dense layers. We already covered Conv2D,
MaxPooling, and Dense layers. In addition, Dropout layers fight with
the overfitting by disregarding some of the neurons while training, while
Flatten layers flatten two-dimensional arrays to a one-dimensional array
before building the fully connected layers.

```
#Importing the required Keras modules containing model and
layers
from tensorflow.keras.models import Sequential
from tensorflow.keras.layers import Dense,Conv2D,
Dropout,Flatten,MaxPooling2D
#Creating a Sequential Model and adding the layers
model = Sequential()
model.add(Conv2D(28,kernel_size=(3,3), input_shape=(28,28,1)))
model.add(MaxPooling2D(pool_size=(2,2))
model.add(Flatten()) #Flattening the 2D arrays for fully
connected layers
model.add(Dense(128,activation=tf.nn.relu))
model.add(Dropout(0.2))
model.add(Dense(10,activation=tf.nn.softmax))
```

We may experiment with any number for the first Dense layer;
however, the final Dense layer must have 10 neurons since we have 10
number classes (0, 1, 2, ..., 9). You may always experiment with kernel size,
pool size, activation functions, dropout rate, and the number of neurons in
the first Dense layer to get a better result.

Compiling and Fitting the Model

With the preceding code, we created a non-optimized empty CNN. Now
it is time to set an optimizer with a given loss function which uses a
metric. Then, we can fit the model by using our train data. We will use the
following code for these tasks and see the outputs shown in Figure 7-7:

```
model.compile(optimizer='adam',
              loss='sparse_categorical_crossentropy',
              metrics=['accuracy'])
model.fit(x=x_train,y=y_train, epochs=10)
```

Output:

```
Epoch 1/10
1875/1875 [==============================] - 31s 17ms/step - loss: 0.2030 - accuracy: 0.9391
Epoch 2/10
1875/1875 [==============================] - 31s 17ms/step - loss: 0.0811 - accuracy: 0.9744
Epoch 3/10
1875/1875 [==============================] - 31s 17ms/step - loss: 0.0550 - accuracy: 0.9822
Epoch 4/10
1875/1875 [==============================] - 32s 17ms/step - loss: 0.0413 - accuracy: 0.9862
Epoch 5/10
1875/1875 [==============================] - 31s 17ms/step - loss: 0.0325 - accuracy: 0.9889
Epoch 6/10
1875/1875 [==============================] - 31s 17ms/step - loss: 0.0271 - accuracy: 0.9910
Epoch 7/10
1875/1875 [==============================] - 31s 17ms/step - loss: 0.0245 - accuracy: 0.9920
Epoch 8/10
1875/1875 [==============================] - 33s 18ms/step - loss: 0.0211 - accuracy: 0.9926
Epoch 9/10
1875/1875 [==============================] - 32s 17ms/step - loss: 0.0197 - accuracy: 0.9932
Epoch 10/10
1875/1875 [==============================] - 31s 17ms/step - loss: 0.0164 - accuracy: 0.9945
<tensorflow.python.keras.callbacks.History at 0x7f1a2a44a550>
```

Figure 7-7. Epoch Stats for Our CNN Training on MNIST Dataset

You can experiment with the optimizer, loss function, metrics, and epochs. However, even though Adam optimizer, categorical crossentropy, and accuracy are the appropriate metrics, feel free to experiment.

Epoch number might seem a bit small. However, you can easily reach to 98–99% test accuracy. Since the MNIST dataset does not require substantial computing power, you may also experiment with the epoch number.

Evaluating the Model

Finally, you may evaluate the trained model with x_test and y_test using a single line of code:

```
model.evaluate(x_test, y_test)
```

The results in Figure 7-8 show the evaluation results for 10 epochs, calculated based on the test set performance.

```
313/313 [==============================] - 2s 7ms/step - loss: 0.0669 - accuracy: 0.9850
[0.06689412891864777, 0.9850000143051147]
```

Figure 7-8. Evaluation Results for Our MNIST-Trained CNN Model with 98.5% Accuracy

We achieved 98.5% accuracy with such a basic model. To be frank, in most image classification cases (e.g., for autonomous cars), we cannot even tolerate a 0.1% error. As an analogy, a 0.1% error can easily mean 1 accident in 1000 cases if we build an autonomous driving system. However, for our very first model, we can say that this result is outstanding.

We can also make individual predictions with the following code:

```
img_pred_index = 1000
plt.imshow(x_test[img_pred_index].reshape(28,28),
        cmap='Greys')
pred = model.predict(
                x_test[img_pred_index].reshape(1,28,28,1))
print("Our CNN model predicts that the digit in the image is:",
pred.argmax())
```

Our trained CNN model will classify the image as the digit "5" (*five*), and here is the visual of the image in Figure 7-9.

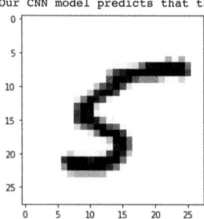

Figure 7-9. *Our Model Correctly Classifies This Image as the Digit 5 (Five)*

Please note that since we shuffle our dataset, you may see a different image for index 1000. But your model still predicts the digit with around 98% accuracy.

Although the image does not have good handwriting of the digit 5 (*five*), our model was able to classify it correctly.

Saving the Trained Model

In this case study, we built our first convolutional neural network to classify handwritten digits with Tensorflow's Keras Sequential API. We achieved an accuracy level of over 98%, and now we can even save this model with the following lines of code:

```
# Save the entire model as a SavedModel.
# Create a 'saved_model' folder under the 'content' folder of
your Google Colab Directory.
!mkdir -p saved_model
# Save the full model with its variables, weights, and biases.
model.save('saved_model/digit_classifier')
```

With the SavedModel, you can rebuild the trained CNN and use it to create different apps such as a digit-classifier game or an image-to-number converter!

Note   There are two types of saving options – the new and fancy "SavedModel" and the old "H5" format. If you would like to learn more about the differences between these formats, please take a look at the Save and Load section of the TensorFlow Guide:

`www.tensorflow.org/tutorials/keras/save_and_load`

Conclusion

Convolutional neural networks are very important and useful neural network models used mainly in image processing and classification. You can detect and classify objects in images, which may be used in many different fields such as anomaly detection in manufacturing, autonomous driving in transportation, and stock management in retail. CNNs are also useful to process audio and video as well as financial data. Therefore, the types of applications that take advantage of CNNs are even broader than the ones mentioned earlier.

CNNs consist of convolutional and pooling layers for feature learning and a set of fully connected layers for prediction and classification. CNNs reduce the complexity of the data, something that feedforward neural networks are not solely capable of.

In the next section, we will cover another essential neural network architecture: recurrent neural networks (RNNs), which are particularly useful for sequence data such as audio, video, text, and time-series data.

CHAPTER 8

Recurrent Neural Networks

In Chapter 6, we covered feedforward neural networks, which are the most basic artificial neural network types. Then, we covered convolutional neural networks in Chapter 7 as the type of artificial neural network architecture, which performs exceptionally good on image data. Now, it is time to cover another type of artificial neural network architecture, recurrent neural network, or RNN, designed particularly to deal with sequential data.

Sequence Data and Time-Series Data

RNNs are extremely useful for sequence data. If you are familiar with predictive analytics, you might know that forecasting with time-series data requires different methods compared to cross-sectional data.

Cross-sectional data refers to a set of observations recorded at a single point in time. The percentage returns of a number of different stocks for this year-end would be an example of cross-sectional data.

Time-series data refers to a set of observations recorded over a given period of time at equally spaced time intervals. The percentage returns of a single stock per year in the last 10 years would be an example of time-series data.

© Orhan Gazi Yalçın 2021
O. G. Yalçın, *Applied Neural Networks with TensorFlow 2*,
https://doi.org/10.1007/978-1-4842-6513-0_8

In time-series datasets, observations are recorded based on a timestamp, but this cannot be generalized to sequence data. Sequence data refers to a broader term. Sequence data is any data where the order of observations matters. So, time series is a particular type of sequence data ordered by timestamps. For example, the order of a sentence (consisting of several words) is essential for its meaning. We cannot just randomly change the order of words and expect it to mean something. However, words in a sentence are not timestamped, so they do not carry any information on time. Therefore, they are only sequence data, not time-series data. Another example of sequence data (but not time-series data) would be a DNA sequence. The order of a DNA sequence is essential, and they are not ordered based on a timestamp. The relationship between sequence data and time-series data is shown in Figure 8-1.

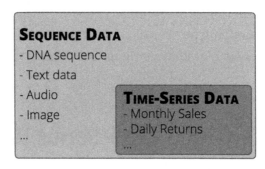

Figure 8-1. *The Relationship Between Sequence Data and Time-Series Data*

Now that you know the relationship between time-series data and – the broader term – sequence data, you also know that when we refer to sequence data, we also refer to time-series data, unless stated otherwise.

RNNs usually do a better job in sequence data problems compared to the alternative neural network architectures. Therefore, it is important to know how to implement recurrent neural networks for sequence data problems such as stock price prediction, sales prediction, DNA sequence modeling, and machine translation.

RNNs and Sequential Data

There are three main limitations of feedforward neural networks which makes them unsuitable for sequence data:

- A feedforward neural network cannot take the order into account.

- A feedforward neural network requires a fixed input size.

- A feedforward neural network cannot output predictions in different lengths.

One of the fundamental characteristics of sequence data is the significance of its order. Rearranging the order of monthly sales can lead us from an increasing trend to a decreasing trend, and our prediction for the next month's sales would change dramatically. This is where the feedforward neural network's limitation surfaces. In a feedforward neural network, the order of the data cannot be taken into account due to this limitation. Rearranging the order of monthly sales would give the exact same result, which proves that they cannot make use of the order of the inputs.

In sequence data studies, the nature of the problems varies, as shown in Figure 8-2. While a machine translation task is a many-to-many problem in nature, sentiment analysis is a many-to-one task. Especially in tasks where many inputs are possible, we often need a variable input size. However, feedforward neural networks require models to be with fixed input size, which makes them unsuitable for many sequence data problems. If the model is trained to make predictions using the last 7 days, you cannot use the 8th day.

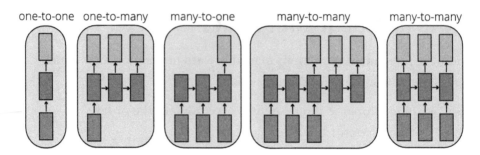

Figure 8-2. *Potential Sequence Data Tasks in Deep Learning*

Finally, a feedforward neural network cannot output different length predictions. Especially in machine translation problems, we cannot predict the size of the output. For instance, a long sentence in English can easily be expressed with a three-word sentence in a different language. This flexibility cannot be provided with a feedforward neural network. But, RNNs provide this capability, and therefore, they are widely used for tasks like machine translation.

The Basics of RNNs

Let's take a quick look at the history of RNNs and then briefly cover the real-world use cases of RNNs and their operating mechanism.

The History of RNNs

We already covered some of the RNNs' history in the previous chapters. The primary motivation to develop RNNs is to eliminate the issues mentioned in the previous section. Over the years, researchers developed different RNN architectures based on their particular research areas. RNNs have many variants, and the total number of different RNN architectures can be expressed in dozens. The first RNN was the Hopfield networks developed by John Hopfield in 1982. In 1997, Hochreiter and Schmidhuber invented long short-term memory (LSTM) networks to address the issues of existing RNNs at the time. LSTM networks perform very well on sequence data tasks, and they are very popular RNN architectures, which are widely used today. In 2014, Kyunghyun Cho introduced recurrent gated units (GRUs) to simplify the LSTM networks. GRUs also perform very well on many tasks, and its inner structure is more straightforward than LSTMs. In this chapter, we will cover simple RNNs, LSTMs, and GRUs in more detail.

Applications of RNNs

There are a significant number of real-world applications of RNNs, and some of these applications can only be built with RNNs. Without RNNs, we would not have competent solutions in many areas, such as machine translation or sentiment analysis. The following is a non-exhaustive list of potential use cases of RNN:

- Grammar learning

- Handwriting recognition

- Human action recognition

- Machine translation

- Music composition

- Predicting subcellular localization of proteins

- Prediction in medical care pathways

- Protein homology detection

- Rhythm learning

- Robotics

- Sentiment analysis

- Speech recognition and synthesis

- Time-series anomaly detection

- Time-series prediction

Mechanism of RNNs

RNNs make use of previous information by keeping them in memory, which is saved as "state" within an RNN neuron.

Before diving into the internal structure of LSTMs and GRUs, let's understand the memory structure with a basic weather forecasting example. We would like to guess if it will rain by using the information provided in a sequence. This sequence of data may be derived from text, speech, or video. After each new information, we slowly update the probability of rainfall and reach a conclusion in the end. Here is the visualization of this task in Figure 8-3.

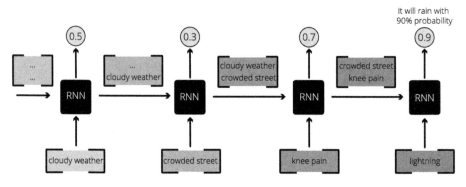

Figure 8-3. *A Simple Weather Forecasting Task: Will It Rain?*

In Figure 8-3, we first record that there is cloudy weather. This single information might be an indication of rain, which calculates into a 50% (or 0.5) probability of rainfall. Then, we receive the following input: crowded street. A crowded street means that people are outside, which means less likelihood of rainfall, and, therefore, our estimation drops to 30% (or 0.3). Then, we are provided with more information: knee pain. It is believed that people with rheumatism feel knee pain before it rains. Therefore, my estimation rises to 70% (or 0.7). Finally, when our model takes lightning as the latest information, the collective estimation increases to 90% (or 0.9). At each time interval, our neuron uses its memory – containing the previous information – and adds the new information on top of this memory to calculate the likelihood of rainfall. The memory structure can be set at the layer level as well as at the cell level. Figure 8-4 shows a cell-level RNN mechanism, (i) folded version on the left and (ii) unfolded version on the right.

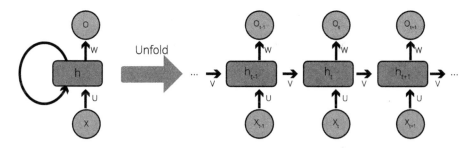

Figure 8-4. *A Cell-Based Recurrent Neural Network Activity*

RNN Types

As mentioned earlier, there are many different variants of RNNs. In this section, we will cover three RNN types we encounter often:

- Simple (Simple) RNN

- Long short-term memory (LSTM) networks

- Gated recurrent unit (GRU) networks

You can find the visualization of these alternative RNN cells in Figure 8-5.

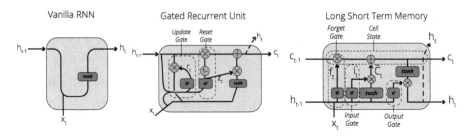

Figure 8-5. *Simple RNN, Gated Recurrent Unit, and Long Short-Term Memory Cells*

As you can see in Figure 8-5, all these three alternatives have common RNN characteristics:

- They all take a t-1 state (memory) into the calculation as a representation of the previous values.

- They all apply some sort of activation functions and do matrix operations.

- They all calculate a current state at time t.

- They repeat this process to perfect their weights and bias values.

Let's examine these three alternatives in detail.

Simple RNNs

Simple RNNs are a network of neuron nodes, which are designed in connected layers. The inner structure of a simple RNN unit is shown in Figure 8-6.

Vanilla RNN

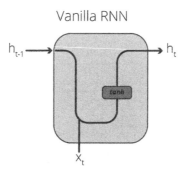

Figure 8-6. *A Simple RNN Unit Structure*

In a simple RNN cell, there are two inputs: (i) the state from the previous time step (t-1) and (ii) the observation at the time t. After an activation function (usually Tanh), the output is passed as the state at the time t to the next cell. Therefore, the effect of the previous information is passed to the next cell at each step.

Simple RNNs can solve many sequence data problems, and they are not computationally intensive. Therefore, it might be the best choice in cases where the resources are limited. It is essential to be aware of simple RNNs; however, it is prone to several technical issues such as vanishing gradient problem. Therefore, we tend to use more complex RNN variants such as long short-term memory (LSTM) and gated recurrent unit (GRU).

Long Short-Term Memory (LSTM)

Long short-term memory (LSTM) networks are invented by Hochreiter and Schmidhuber in 1997 and improved the highest accuracy performances in many different applications, which are designed to solve sequence data problems.

An LSTM unit consists of a cell state, an input gate, an output gate, and a forget gate, as shown in Figure 8-7. These three gates regulate the flow of information into and out of the LSTM unit. In addition, LSTM units have both a cell state and a hidden state.

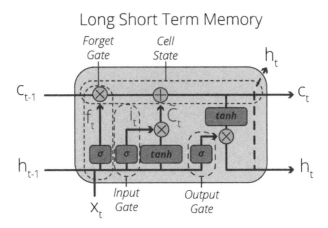

Figure 8-7. *A Long Short-Term Memory Unit Structure*

LSTM networks are well suited for sequence data problems in any format, and they are less prone to vanishing gradient problems, which are common in simple RNN networks. On the other hand, we might still encounter with exploding gradient problem, where the gradients go to the infinity. Another downside of LSTM networks is their computationally intensive nature. Training a model using LSTM might take a lot of time and processing power, which is the main reason why GRUs are developed.

Gated Recurrent Units (GRUs)

Gated recurrent units are introduced in 2014 by Kyunghyun Cho. Just as LSTMs, GRUs are also gating mechanism in RNNs to deal with sequence data. However, to simplify the calculation process, GRUs use two gates: (i) reset gate and (ii) update gate. GRUs also use the same values for hidden state and cell state. Figure 8-8 shows the inner structure of a gated recurrent unit.

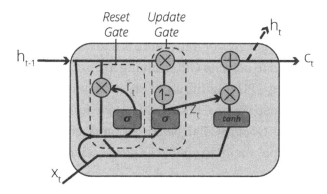

Figure 8-8. *A Gated Recurrent Unit Structure*

GRUs are useful when computational resources are limited. Even though GRUs outperform LSTMs in some applications, LSTMs usually outperform GRUs. A good strategy when dealing with sequence data to train two models with LSTM and GRU and select the best performing one since the performance of these two alternative gating mechanisms can change case by case.

Case Study I Sentiment Analysis with IMDB Reviews

Now that we covered the conceptual part of recurrent neural networks, it is time for a case study. In general, you don't have to memorize the inner working structure for simple RNNs, LSTMs, and GRUs to build recurrent neural networks. TensorFlow APIs make it very easy to build RNNs that do well on several tasks. In this section, we will conduct a sentiment analysis case study with the IMDB reviews database, which is inspired by TensorFlow's official tutorial, titled "Text Classification with an RNN".[1]

---

[1]Text classification with an RNN, TensorFlow, available at www.tensorflow.org/tutorials/text/text_classification_rnn

Preparing Our Colab for GPU Accelerated Training

Before diving into exploring our data, there is one crucial environment adjustment: we need to activate GPU training in our Google Colab Notebook. Activating GPU training is a fairly straightforward task, but failure to do it will keep you in CPU training mode forever.

Please go to your Google Colab Notebook, and select the Runtime ➤ "Change runtime type" menu to enable a GPU accelerator, as shown in Figure 8-9.

As mentioned in earlier chapters, using a GPU or TPU – instead of a CPU – for training usually speeds up the training. Now that we enabled GPU use in our model, we can confirm whether a GPU is activated for training with the following code:

```
import tensorflow as tf
print("Num GPUs Available: ", len(tf.config.experimental.list_
physical_devices('GPU')))
```

Output: Num GPUs Available: 1

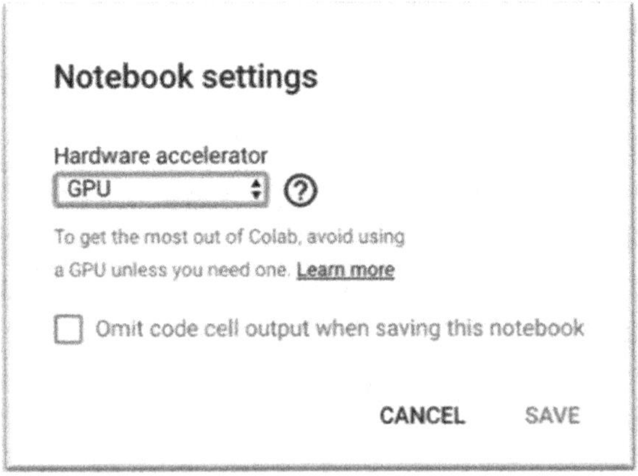

Figure 8-9. Enabling GPU Acceleration in Google Colab

IMDB Reviews

IMDB reviews dataset is a large movie review dataset collected and prepared by Andrew L. Maas from the popular movie rating service, IMDB.[2] IMDB reviews is used for binary sentiment classification, whether a review is positive or negative. IMDB reviews contains 25,000 movie reviews for training and 25,000 for testing. All these 50,000 reviews are labeled data that may be used for supervised deep learning. Besides, there is an additional 50,000 unlabeled reviews that we will not use in this case study.

Lucky for us, TensorFlow already processed the raw text data and prepared us a bag-of-words format. In addition, we also have access to the raw text. Preparing the bag of words is a natural language processing (NLP) task, which we will cover in the upcoming Chapter 9. Therefore, in this example, we will barely use any NLP technique. Instead, we will use the processed bag-of-words version so that we can easily build our RNN model to predict whether a review is positive or negative.

TensorFlow Imports for Dataset Downloading

We start with two initial imports that are the main TensorFlow import and the TensorFlow datasets import to load the data:

```
import tensorflow as tf
import tensorflow_datasets as tfds
```

---

[2]Andrew L. Maas, Raymond E. Daly, Peter T. Pham, Dan Huang, Andrew Y. Ng, and Christopher Potts. (2011). Learning Word Vectors for Sentiment Analysis. The 49th Annual Meeting of the Association for Computational Linguistics (ACL 2011).

Loading the Dataset from TensorFlow

TensorFlow offers several popular datasets, which can directly be loaded from the `tensorflow_datasets` API. The `load()` function of the `tensorflow_datasets` API returns two objects: (i) a dictionary containing train, test, and unlabeled sets and (ii) information and other relevant objects regarding the IMDB reviews dataset. We can save them as variables with the following code:

```
# Dataset is a dictionary containing train, test, and unlabeled
datasets
# Info contains relevant information about the dataset
dataset, info = tfds.load('imdb_reviews/subwords8k',
                          with_info=True,
                          as_supervised=True)
```

Understanding the Bag-of-Word Concept: Text Encoding and Decoding

A bag of words is a representation of text that describes the occurrence of words within a document. This representation is created based on a vocabulary of words. In our dataset, reviews are encoded using a vocabulary of 8185 words. We can access the encoder via the "info" object that we created earlier.

```
# Using info we can load the encoder which converts text to bag
of words
encoder = info.features['text'].encoder
print('Vocabulary size: {}'.format(encoder.vocab_size))
```
output: Vocabulary size: 8185

By using this encoder, we can encode new reviews:

```
# You can also encode a brand new comment with encode function
```

```
review = 'Terrible Movie!.'
encoded_review = encoder.encode(review)
print('Encoded review is {}'.format(encoded_review))
```

output: Encoded review is [3585, 3194, 7785, 7962, 7975]

We can also decode an encoded review as follows:

```
# You can easily decode an encoded review with decode function
original_review = encoder.decode(encoded_review)
print('The original review is "{}"'.format(original_review))
```

output: The original review is "Terrible Movie!."

Preparing the Dataset

We already saved our reviews in the "dataset" object, which is a dictionary with three keys: (i) train, (ii) test, and (iii) unlabeled. By using these keys, we will split our train and test sets with the following code:

```
# We can easily split our dataset dictionary with the relevant keys
train_dataset, test_dataset = dataset['train'], dataset['test']
```

We also need to shuffle our dataset to avoid any bias and pad our reviews so that all of them are in the same length. We need to select a large buffer size so that we can have a well-mixed train dataset. In addition, to avoid the excessive computational burden, we will limit our sequence length to 64.

```
BUFFER_SIZE = 10000
BATCH_SIZE = 64

train_dataset = train_dataset.shuffle(BUFFER_SIZE)
train_dataset = train_dataset.padded_batch(BATCH_SIZE)
test_dataset = test_dataset.padded_batch(BATCH_SIZE)
```

175

Padding   Padding is a useful method to encode sequence data into contiguous batches. To be able to fit all the sequences to a defined length, we must pad or truncate some sequences in our dataset.

Building the Recurrent Neural Network

Now that our train and test datasets are ready to be fed into the model, we can start building our RNN model with LSTM units.

Imports for Model Building

We use Keras Sequential API to build our models. We also need Dense, Embedding, Bidirectional, LSTM, and Dropout layers to build our RNN model. We also need to import Binary Crossentropy as our loss function since we use binary classification to predict whether a comment is negative or positive. Finally, we use Adam optimizer to optimize our weights with backpropagation. These components are imported with the following lines of code:

```
from tensorflow.keras.models import Sequential
from tensorflow.keras.layers import (Dense,
                                      Embedding,
                                      Bidirectional,
                                      Dropout,
                                      LSTM)
from tensorflow.keras.losses import BinaryCrossentropy
from tensorflow.keras.optimizers import Adam
```

Create the Model and Fill It with Layers

We use an Encoding layer, two LSTM layers wrapped in Bidirectional layers, two Dense layers, and a Dropout layer. We start with an embedding layer, which converts the sequences of word indices to sequences of vectors.

An embedding layer stores one vector per word. Then, we add two LSTM layers wrapped in Bidirectional layers. Bidirectional layers propagate the input back and forth through the LSTM layers and then concatenate the output, which is useful to learn long-range dependencies. Then, we add to one Dense layer with 64 neurons to increase the complexity, a Dropout layer to fight overfitting. Finally, we add a final Dense layer to make a binary prediction. The following lines of code create a Sequential model and add all the mentioned layers:

```
model = Sequential([
    Embedding(encoder.vocab_size, 64),
    Bidirectional(LSTM(64,  return_sequences=True)),
    Bidirectional(LSTM(32)),
    Dense(64, activation='relu'),
    Dropout(0.5),
    Dense(1)
])
```

As shown in Figure 8-10, we can also see the overview of the model with `model.summary()`.

```
Model: "sequential"
_____
Layer (type)                 Output Shape              Param #
=================================================================
embedding (Embedding)        (None, None, 64)          523840
_____
bidirectional (Bidirectional (None, None, 128)         66048
_____
bidirectional_1 (Bidirection (None, 64)                41216
_____
dense (Dense)                (None, 64)                4160
_____
dropout (Dropout)            (None, 64)                0
_____
dense_1 (Dense)              (None, 1)                 65
=================================================================
Total params: 635,329
Trainable params: 635,329
Non-trainable params: 0
_____
```

Figure 8-10. *The Summary of the RNN Model*

We can also create a flowchart of our RNN model, as you can see in Figure 8-11, with the following line:

```
tf.keras.utils.plot_model(model)
```

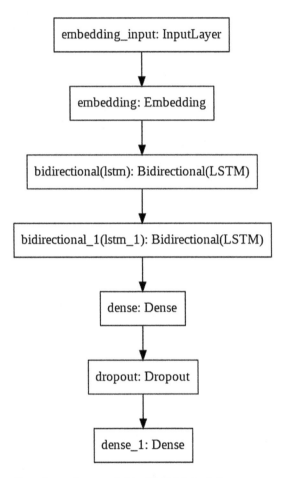

Figure 8-11. *The Flowchart of the RNN Model*

Compiling and Fitting the Model

Now that we build an empty model, it is time to configure the loss function, optimizer, and performance metrics with the following code:

```
model.compile(
loss=BinaryCrossentropy(from_logits=True),
      optimizer=Adam(1e-4),
      metrics=['accuracy'])
```

Our data and model are ready for training. We can use `model.fit()` function to train our model. Around 10 epochs would be more than enough for training our sentiment analysis model, which may take around 30 minutes. We also save our training process as a variable to access the performance of the model over time.

```
history = model.fit(train_dataset, epochs=10,
                    validation_data=test_dataset,
                    validation_steps=30)
```

Figure 8-12 shows the main performance measures at each epoch.

```
Epoch 1/10
391/391 [==============================] - 238s 608ms/step - loss: 0.6582 - accuracy: 0.5545 - val_loss: 0.5013 - val_accuracy: 0.7568
Epoch 2/10
391/391 [==============================] - 237s 607ms/step - loss: 0.3752 - accuracy: 0.8450 - val_loss: 0.3624 - val_accuracy: 0.8510
Epoch 3/10
391/391 [==============================] - 236s 603ms/step - loss: 0.2653 - accuracy: 0.9037 - val_loss: 0.3619 - val_accuracy: 0.8479
Epoch 4/10
391/391 [==============================] - 236s 604ms/step - loss: 0.2185 - accuracy: 0.9260 - val_loss: 0.3627 - val_accuracy: 0.8562
Epoch 5/10
391/391 [==============================] - 236s 603ms/step - loss: 0.1852 - accuracy: 0.9400 - val_loss: 0.3955 - val_accuracy: 0.8516
Epoch 6/10
391/391 [==============================] - 235s 602ms/step - loss: 0.1542 - accuracy: 0.9541 - val_loss: 0.4103 - val_accuracy: 0.8630
Epoch 7/10
391/391 [==============================] - 236s 603ms/step - loss: 0.1307 - accuracy: 0.9618 - val_loss: 0.4841 - val_accuracy: 0.8490
Epoch 8/10
391/391 [==============================] - 237s 606ms/step - loss: 0.1260 - accuracy: 0.9621 - val_loss: 0.4424 - val_accuracy: 0.8458
Epoch 9/10
391/391 [==============================] - 237s 605ms/step - loss: 0.1004 - accuracy: 0.9735 - val_loss: 0.5077 - val_accuracy: 0.8562
Epoch 10/10
391/391 [==============================] - 235s 602ms/step - loss: 0.0933 - accuracy: 0.9759 - val_loss: 0.5068 - val_accuracy: 0.8469
```

Figure 8-12. *Model Training Performance at Each Epoch*

Evaluating the Model

After seeing an accuracy performance of around 85%, we can safely move on to evaluating our model. We use `test_dataset` to calculate our final loss and accuracy values:

```
test_loss, test_acc = model.evaluate(test_dataset)

print('Test Loss: {}'.format(test_loss))
print('Test Accuracy: {}'.format(test_acc))
```

After running the code above, we get the output shown below in Figure 8-13:

```
391/391 [==============================] - 94s 240ms/step - loss: 0.3392 - accuracy: 0.8648
Test Loss: 0.3391561210155487
Test Accuracy: 0.8647599816322327
```

Figure 8-13. *Model Evaluation After Training*

We can also use our history object to plot the performance measures over time with the following code:

```
import matplotlib.pyplot as plt

def plot_graphs(history, metric):
  plt.plot(history.history[metric])
  plt.plot(history.history['val_'+metric], '')
  plt.xlabel("Epochs")
  plt.ylabel(metric)
  plt.legend([metric, 'val_'+metric])
  plt.show()
plot_graphs(history, 'accuracy')
```

Figure 8-14 shows the plot outputted.

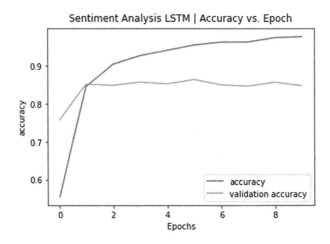

Figure 8-14. *Accuracy vs. Epoch Plot for Sentiment Analysis LSTM Model*

Making New Predictions

Now that we trained our RNN model, we can make new sentiment predictions from the reviews our model has never seen before. Since we encoded and pad our train and test set, we have to process new reviews the same way. Therefore, we need a padder and an encoder. The following code is our custom padding function:

```
def review_padding(encoded_review, padding_size):
  zeros = [0] * (padding_size - len(encoded_review))
  encoded_review.extend(zeros)
  return encoded_review
```

We also need an encoder function that would encode and process our review to feed into our trained model. The following function completes these tasks:

```
def review_encoder(review):
        encoded_review = review_padding(encoder.encode( review ),
        64)
        encoded_review = tf.cast( encoded_review,  tf.float32)
        return tf.expand_dims( encoded_review, 0)
```

Now we can easily make predictions from previously unseen reviews. For this task, I visited the page IMDB reviews on the movie Fight Club and selected the following comment:

```
fight_club_review = 'It has some cliched moments, even for its
time, but FIGHT CLUB is an awesome film. I have watched it
about 100 times in the past 20 years. It never gets old. It
is hard to discuss this film without giving things away but
suffice it to say, it is a great thriller with some intriguing
twists.'
```

The reviewer gave 8-star and wrote this comment for Fight Club. Therefore, it is clearly a positive comment. Thanks to the custom functions we defined earlier, making a new prediction is very easy, as shown in the following line:

```
model.predict(review_encoder(fight_club_review))
```

output: array([[1.5780725]], dtype=float32)

When the output is larger than 0.5, our model classifies the review as positive, whereas negative if below 0.5. Since our output is 1.57, we confirm that our model successfully predicts the sentiment of the review.

Although our model has more than 85% accuracy, one bias I recognized is with regard to the length of the review. When we select a very short review, no matter how positive it is, we always get a negative result. This issue can be addressed with fine-tuning. Even though we will not conduct fine-tuning in this case study, feel free to work on it to improve the model even further.

Saving and Loading the Model

You have successfully trained an RNN model, and you can finish this chapter. But I would like to cover one more topic: saving and loading the trained model. As you experienced, training this model took about 30 minutes, and Google Colab deletes everything you have done after some time of inactivity. So, you have to save your trained model for later use. Besides, you cannot simply save it to a Google Colab directory because it is also deleted after a while. The solution is to save it to your Google Drive. To be able to use our model at any time over the cloud, we should

- Give Colab access to save files to our Google Drive

- Save the trained model to the designated path

- Load the trained model from Google Drive at any time

- Make predictions with the SavedModel object

Give Colab Access to Google Drive

To be able to give access to Colab, we need to run the following code inside our Colab Notebook:

```
from google.colab import drive
drive.mount('/content/gdrive')
```

Follow the instructions in the output cell to complete this task.

Save Trained Model to Google Drive

Now that we can access our Google Drive files from Colab Notebooks, we can create a new folder called saved_models and save our SavedModel object to this folder with the following lines of code:

```
# This will create a 'saved_model' folder under the 'content'
folder.
!mkdir -p "/content/gdrive/My Drive/saved_model"
# This will save the full model with its variables, weights,
and biases.
model.save('/content/gdrive/My Drive/saved_model/sentiment_
analysis')
# Also save the encoder for later use
  encoder.save_to_file('/content/gdrive/My Drive/saved_model/
  sa_vocab')
```

After this code, we can load our trained model as long as we keep the saved files in our Google Drive. You can also view the folders and files under the sentiment_analysis folder with the following code:

```
import os
os.listdir("/content/gdrive/My Drive/saved_model/sentiment_
analysis")
```
output: ['variables', 'assets', 'saved_model.pb']

Load the Trained Model and Make Predictions

To be able to load the saved_model, we can use the load attribute of the saved_model object. We just need to pass the exact path that our model is located (*make sure Colab has access to your Google Drive*), and as soon as we run the code, our model is ready for use:

```
import tensorflow as tf
loaded = tf.keras.models.load_model("/content/gdrive/My Drive/
saved_model/sentiment_analysis/")
```

We also load our previously saved vocabulary list for encoding and decoding with the following code:

```
import tensorflow_datasets as tfds
vocab_path = '/content/gdrive/My Drive/saved_model/sa_vocab'
encoder = tfds.features.text.SubwordTextEncoder.load_from_
file(vocab_path)
```

Also, make sure you run the cells where review_padding() and review_encoder() functions (shared earlier) are defined once more if you restart your runtime.

Note that the loaded model object is exactly the same as our previous model, and it has the standard model functions like as fit(), evaluate(), and predict(). To be able to make predictions, we need to use the predict() function of our loaded model object. We also need to pass our processed review as the embedding_input argument. The following line of code completes these tasks:

184

```
fight_club_review = 'It has some cliched moments, even for its
time, but FIGHT CLUB is an awesome film. I have watched it
about 100 times in the past 20 years. It never gets old. It
is hard to discuss this film without giving things away but
suffice it to say, it is a great thriller with some intriguing
twists.'
```

```
loaded.predict(review_encoder(rev))
```
output: array([[1.5780725]], dtype=float32)

As expected, we get the same output. Therefore, we successfully saved our model, load it, and make predictions. Now you can embed this trained model to a web app, REST API, or mobile app to serve to the world!

Conclusion

In this chapter, we covered recurrent neural networks, a type of artificial neural network, which is designed particularly to deal with sequential data. We covered the basics of RNNs and different types of RNNs (basic RNN, LSTM, GRU neurons). Then, we conducted a case study using the IMDB reviews dataset. Our RNN learned to predict whether a review is positive or negative (i.e., sentiment analysis) by using more than 50,000 reviews.

In the next chapter, we will cover natural language processing, a subfield of artificial intelligence, which deals with text data. In addition, we will build another RNN model in the next chapter, but this time, it will generate text data.

## CHAPTER 9

Natural Language Processing

Natural language processing (NLP) is an interdisciplinary subfield, which has components from major fields such as linguistics, computer science, and artificial intelligence. NLP is mainly concerned with the interaction between humans and computers. The scope of NLP ranges from computational understanding and generation of human languages to processing and analyzing large amounts of natural language data. The scope of NLP also contains text, speech, cognition, and their interactions. In this chapter, we briefly cover the history of NLP, the differences between rule-based NLP and statistical NLP, and the major NLP methods and techniques. We finally conduct a case study on NLP to prepare you for real-world problems.

History of NLP

The history of NLP can be split into four major eras:

- Early ideas era

- Rule-based NLP era

- Statistical NLP with supervised learning era

- Unsupervised and semi-supervised learning era

© Orhan Gazi Yalçın 2021
O. G. Yalçın, *Applied Neural Networks with TensorFlow 2*,
https://doi.org/10.1007/978-1-4842-6513-0_9

Note that these eras are complementary, rather than disruptive. Therefore, we still take advantage of the rules and methods introduced since the early eras.

Early Ideas

The history of natural language processing starts in the 17th century with the philosophical proposals by Leibniz and Descartes to introduce special codes that would connect words between different languages. Even though these proposals always remain in the theoretical side, they influence the scientists in the upcoming centuries to realize the idea of automated machine translation.

Rule-Based NLP

The common nature of this era is the heavy use of complex handwritten rules to cover potential outcomes of NLP tasks. The very early NLP-related innovations were first observed with the patents for "translating machines" in the 1930s. These early patents contain automated bilingual dictionaries and methods to deal with the grammatical rules between languages.

During World War II, machine translating devices were developed to translate communications between enemy lines. However, these machines were mostly unsuccessful.

As in all the other fields of artificial intelligence, in 1950, Turing Test sets the criteria for intelligence, which include understanding conversations in natural languages.

In 1957, Noam Chomsky announced Syntactic Structures, a rule-based system, which revolutionized linguistic studies with a universal grammar rule.

In 1954, with the Georgetown experiment, 60 sentences in Russian were automatically translated into English. This successful experiment encouraged the authors to claim that the machine translation between these two languages would be accomplished within 3 to 5 years. This positive approach was in line with the other artificial intelligence subfields, where most of these optimistic promises were failed to be realized. Therefore, the funds were cut for NLP studies in the late 1960s and the early 1970s, during the era of the AI winter.

Despite limited funding, some successful NLP systems were developed in the 1960s, working in restricted environments. The 1970s were the years when many programmers began to write "conceptual ontologies," which structure, group, and sort real-world objects into binary data.

Statistical NLP and Supervised Learning

Around the 1980s, the steady increase in computing power and the popularization of corpus linguistics that prioritizes the machine learning approach to language processing made it possible to use statistical models in NLP. Although the early studies in statistical NLPs were not much different than the rule-based NLP studies, with the introduction of more complex methods, statistical NLP has become more probabilistic. This shift from ruled-based models to statistical models increased the accuracy performance, especially for unusual observations.

In this era, IBM Research has taken the lead and developed several successful NLP solutions such as IBM Watson. Also, the multilingual official documents produced by the European Union, the United Nations, and the Parliament of Canada have contributed to the development of successful machine translation systems.

On the other hand, smaller players with limited access to these large text corpora focused on developing methods that can effectively learn from a limited amount of data.

Unsupervised and Semi-supervised NLP

Today, the real-world applications of NLP problems are becoming more and more successful. However, finding enough labeled data is one of the major problems observed in modern NLP research. Therefore, using unsupervised and semi-supervised learning algorithms for common NLP tasks has become increasingly more popular. Generally speaking, predictions made with unsupervised learning algorithms are less accurate than their supervised counterparts. However, with unsupervised models, researchers can infer results from enormously large sizes of data, which are very useful for discovering more complex patterns.

Real-World Applications of NLP

The number of NLP real-world applications is increasing with advancements in the field of machine learning. With the increased computing power, a number of available machine learning models, and the availability of a vast amount of text corpora, a new use case for NLP is discovered every day. Here is a list of the most popular NLP applications:

- **Machine Translation**: The task of translating text from one language to text in another language (e.g., Google Translate)

- **Speech Recognition**: The task of recognizing human voice to take actions or to convert into text

- **Sentiment Analysis**: The task of understanding the emotion in a text piece, such as a review

- **Question Answering**: The task of developing systems that can accurately deliver an answer to a given question (e.g., Siri)

- **Automatic Summarization**: The task of deriving a short summary from a full text without losing the significant points

- **Chatbots**: The task of developing special systems capable of several NLP tasks such as question answering, speech recognition, and more

- **Market Intelligence**: The task of analyzing customer behavior by taking advantage of several NLP and other statistical methods

- **Text Classification**: The task of classifying texts into given classes by analyzing their contents, structures, and other relevant features

- **Optical Character Recognition (OCR)**: The task of analyzing image data and converting it to text with the help of computer vision and image processing methods

- **Spell Checking**: The task of identifying and correcting spelling mistakes in a text (e.g., Grammarly)

To be able to develop these real-world applications, researchers have to use several NLP methods that are covered in the next section.

Major Evaluations, Techniques, Methods, and Tasks

Processing of natural language data consists of several small tasks which may be grouped into the following groups:

- Morphosyntax

- Semantics

- Discourse

- Speech

- Dialogue

- Cognition

In the following section, we will cover these tasks under their corresponding groups.

Morphosyntax

Morphosyntax is the study of grammatical categories and linguistic units created based on morphological and syntactic properties. In the field of NLP, there are a number of essential morphosyntactic tasks which are listed as follows:

- **Base Form Extraction: There are two popular methods to extract the base form of words.**

  - **Lemmatization**: Removing the insignificant endings of words and returning their base dictionary form (i.e., lemma) by using an actual dictionary (e.g., converting *swimming* to *swim* by removing the -*ing* suffix).

  - **Stemming**: A method to reduce inflected or derived words to their root form. Although stemming is similar to lemmatization, the root form generated using stemming does not have to be a real word (e.g., the words *trouble, troubling,* and *troubled* are stemmed into *troubl*).

- **Grammar Induction**: Generating a language-wide formal grammar that describes its syntax.

- **Morphological Segmentation**: Separating words into the smallest meaningful units (i.e., *morphemes*) and identifying the classes of these units.

- **Part-of-Speech (POS) Tagging**: Determining the POS type for each word. The common POS types are noun, verb, adjective, adverb, pronoun, preposition, conjunction, interjection, numeral, article, or determiner.

- **Parsing**: Determining the parse tree of a given string (e.g., a sentence). A parse tree is an ordered, rooted tree, which represents the syntactic structure of a string.

- **Sentence Breaking**: Finding the sentence boundaries. Several punctuation marks such as periods or exclamation points are useful for this task.

- **Word Segmentation**: Separating a given text into separate words. This process is often used to create a bag of words (BOW) and **text vectorization**.

- **Terminology Extraction**: Extracting relevant terms from a given corpus.

Semantics

Semantics is an interdisciplinary field in the intersection of linguistics and logic concerned with meaning. While logical semantics is concerned with sense, reference, and implication, lexical semantics is concerned with the analysis of word meanings and relations between them. The main problems, methods, and tasks related to semantics are as follows:

- **Machine Translation**: As explained earlier, an automatic translation of text from one human language to another.

- **Named Entity Recognition (NER)**: Finding the people and place names in a given string. While capitalization is useful for NER, there is certainly much more work involved.

- **Natural Language Generation**: Generating text in natural languages using word representations and statistical models.

- **Optical Character Recognition**: As explained earlier, identifying the text data from an image containing printed text.

- **Question Answering**: As explained previously, given a question in a natural language, providing an answer.

- **Recognizing Textual Entailment**: Identifying a directional relation between text fragments, which is more relaxed than rigid logical entailment.

An example of positive textual entailment between two strings is as follows:

Text: If you work hard, you will be successful.

Hypothesis: Hardworking has good consequences.

- **Relationship Extraction**: Identifying real-world relations from a given text (e.g., Person A works for Company X).

- **Sentiment Analysis**: As explained previously, extracting subjective information (i.e., emotions) from a set of documents.

- **Topic Segmentation and Recognition**: Classifying a set of documents or text into separate topics. While the topic boundaries may be apparent in some cases, usually it requires more evaluation.

- **Word Sense Disambiguation**: Determining the meaning of a word with more than one meaning based on the context.

Discourse

- **Automatic Summarization**: As explained earlier, producing a readable summary of a large text.

- **Coreference Resolution**: Determining which words refer to the same objects, which include nouns as well as pronouns. Coreference occurs when more than one expression in a text refer to the same object.

- **Discourse Analysis**: The study of written or spoken language in relation to its social context, which aims to understand how language is used in real-life situations.

Speech

- **Speech Recognition**: As explained earlier, converting a given sound clip of a person speaking into the text

- **Speech Segmentation**: A subtask of speech recognition, separating the recognized text into words

- **Text-to-Speech**: Converting a given text to its audio representation

Dialogue

Initiating and continuing a meaningful written or spoken conversational exchange with a human or a machine. Dialogue requires simultaneous completion of several tasks such as answering questions, text-to-speech, speech recognition, sentiment analysis, and more.

Cognition

Acquiring knowledge and understanding through thought, experience, and senses. It is regarded as the most complex evaluation of NLP and usually referred to as natural language understanding (NLU).

Natural Language Toolkit (NLTK)

NLTK is an essential Python library designated for NLP tasks. NLTK supports essential NLP tasks such as text classification, stemming and lemmatization, tagging, parsing, tokenization, and even reasoning.

After being developed by Steven Bird and Edward Loper at the University of Pennsylvania, NLTK is regarded as the main NLP library for Python.

Even though you can take advantage of data science libraries such as Pandas, scikit-learn, TensorFlow, and NumPy, the methods available in these libraries cannot even be compared with what NLTK offers.

Available NLTK Modules are listed here.

app	parse
ccg	probability
chat	sem
chunk	sentiment
classify	stem
cluster	tag
collections	tbl
corpus	test
data	text
downloader	tokenize
draw	toolbox
featstruct	translate
grammar	tree
help	treetransform
inference	twitter
lm	util
metrics	wsd
misc	

Useful Information About NLTK

- **Website**: www.nltk.org/

- **Documentation URL for Modules**: www.nltk.org/py-modindex

- **Installation command**: pip install --user -U nltk

- **Preferred Alias for Importing**: import nltk

197

Case Study | Text Generation with Deep NLP

Note that the topic of NLP is an expertise area by itself. Someone can spend an entire life working on NLP studies. In this chapter, we only make an introduction, and now that we covered the main topics in natural language processing, we can move on to our case study: text generation with deep natural language processing.

One of the most important topics in NLP projects is text vectorization. In this case study, we will refer to Andrej Karpathy's blog post, "The Unreasonable Effectiveness of Recurrent Neural Networks"[1], and TensorFlow Team's take on this post[2].

The research has shown that one of the most effective artificial neural network types for NLP is recurrent neural networks (RNNs). RNNs are widely used in NLP tasks such as machine translation, text generation, and image captioning. In NLP tasks, generally, a developer uses NLP tools and methods to process the text data into vectors and then feed them into a selected artificial neural network such as RNN, CNN, or even feedforward neural network to complete a task. In our case study, we also follow these two standardized steps: (i) process the text into vectors and (ii) train a neural network with these vectors.

The Goal of the Case Study

It is crucial to fully understand the goal of the case study. In this case study, our goal is to train an RNN, which is capable of generating meaningful text using characters. An RNN can generate text from words as well as from characters, and we select to use characters to generate text for this

---

[1]The Unreasonable Effectiveness of Recurrent Neural Networks, available on http://karpathy.github.io/2015/05/21/rnn-effectiveness

[2]Text generation with an RNN | TensorFlow Core TensorFlow, available on www.tensorflow.org/tutorials/text/text_generation

case study. The problem is when we build a new RNN with no training, it combines a bunch of meaningless characters, which does not mean anything. However, if we feed our RNN with a lot of text data, it starts to imitate the style of these texts and generate meaningful text using characters. So, if we feed the model a lot of didactic text, our model would generate educational materials. If we feed our model with lots of poems, our model will start generating poems, so we would end up having an artificial poet. These are all viable options, but we will feed our model with something else: a long text dataset containing Shakespeare's writings. Therefore, we will create an artificial Shakespeare.

Shakespeare Corpus

Shakespeare Corpus is a text file containing 40,000 lines of Shakespeare's writing, which is cleaned and prepared by Karpathy and hosted by TensorFlow team on this URL:

```
https://storage.googleapis.com/download.tensorflow.org/data/
shakespeare.txt
```

I strongly recommend you take a look at the .txt file to understand the text we are dealing with. The file contains the conversational content where each character's name is placed before the corresponding part, as shown in Figure 9-1.

```
KATHARINA:
So may you lose your arms:
If you strike me, you are no gentleman;
And if no gentleman, why then no arms.

PETRUCHIO:
A herald, Kate? O, put me in thy books!

KATHARINA:
What is your crest? a coxcomb?

PETRUCHIO:
A combless cock, so Kate will be my hen.

KATHARINA:
No cock of mine; you crow too like a craven.

PETRUCHIO:
Nay, come, Kate, come; you must not look so sour.
```

Figure 9-1. *A Part from the Shakespeare Corpus*

Initial Imports

In this case study, the required libraries are TensorFlow, NumPy, and os, which we can import them with the following code:

```
import tensorflow as tf
import numpy as np
import os
```

Did you notice that I did not mention the NLTK library? The reason for this is that TensorFlow also offers limited support for NLP tasks, and in this case study, coupled with NumPy operations, we are capable of vectorizing our dataset with TensorFlow. The main reason for this is that our corpus is pretty much standardized and cleaned. If we needed a more complex NLP method, we would have had to rely on NLTK, Pandas, and NumPy libraries to a greater extent.

Loading the Corpus

To be able to load a dataset from an online directory, we can use the util module of the Keras API in TensorFlow. For this task, we will use the get_file() function, which downloads a file from a URL if it not already in the cache, with the following code:

```
path_to_file = tf.keras.utils.get_file('shakespeare.txt',
'https://storage.googleapis.com/download.tensorflow.org/data/
shakespeare.txt')
```

After downloading our file, we can open the file from the cache with the following Python code:

```
text = open(path_to_file, 'rb').read()
text = text.decode(encoding='utf-8')
```

Now, we successfully saved the entire corpus in the Colab notebook's memory as a variable. Let's see how many characters there in the corpus are and what's the first 100 characters, with the following code:

```
print ('Total number of characters in the corpus is:',
len(text))
print('The first 100 characters of the corpus are as
follows:\n', text[:100])
```
Output:
```
Total number of characters in the corpus is: 1115394
The first 100 characters of the corpus are as follows:
 First Citizen:
Before we proceed any further, hear me speak.

All:
Speak, speak.

First Citizen:
You
```

Our entire corpus is accessible via a Python variable, named *text*, and now we can start vectorizing it.

Vectorize the Text

Text vectorization is a fundamental NLP method to transform text data into a meaningful vector of numbers so that a machine can understand. There are various approaches to text vectorization. In this case study, step by step, this is how we go about this:

- Give an index number to each unique character.

- Run a for loop in the corpus, and index every character in the whole text.

To assign an index number to each unique character, we first have to create a list containing only a single copies of all the unique characters in the text. This is very easy with the built-in set() function, which converts a list object to a set object only with unique values.

The difference between set and list data structures is that lists are ordered and allow duplicates, while sets are unordered and don't allow duplicate elements. So, when we run the set() function, as shown in the following code, it returns a set of unique characters in the text file:

```
vocab = sorted(set(text))
print ('The number of unique characters in the corpus is',
len(vocab))
print('A slice of the unique characters set:\n', vocab[:10])
```
Output:
```
The number of unique characters in the corpus is 65
A slice of the unique characters set:
 ['\n', ' ', '!', '$', '&', "'", ',', '-', '.', '3']
```

We also need to give each character an index number. The following code assigns a number to each set item and then creates a dictionary of the set items with their given numbers with the following code:

```
char2idx = {u:i for i, u in enumerate(vocab)}
```

We also make a copy of the unique set elements in NumPy array format for later use in decoding the predictions:

```
idx2char = np.array(vocab)
```

Now we can vectorize our text with a simple for loop where we go through each character in the text and assign their corresponding index value and save all the index values as a new list, with the following code:

```
text_as_int = np.array([char2idx[c] for c in text])
```

Creating the Dataset

At this point, we have our char2idx dictionary to vectorize the text and idx2char to de-vectorize (i.e., decode) the vectorized text. Finally, we have our text_as_int as our vectorized NumPy array. We can now create our dataset.

Firstly, we will use from_tensor_slices method from Dataset module to create a TensorFlow Dataset object from our text_as_int object, and we will split them into batches. The length of each input of the dataset is limited to 100 characters. We can achieve all of them with the following code:

```
char_dataset = tf.data.Dataset.from_tensor_slices(text_as_int)
seq_length = 100 # The max. length for single input
sequences = char_dataset.batch(seq_length+1, drop_
remainder=True)
```

Our sequences object contains sequences of characters, but we have to create a tuple of these sequences simply to feed into the RNN model. We can achieve this with the custom mapping function as follows:

```
def split_input_target(chunk):
    input_text = chunk[:-1]
    target_text = chunk[1:]
    return input_text, target_text

dataset = sequences.map(split_input_target)
```

The reason that we generated these tuples is that for RNN to work, we need to create a pipeline, as shown in Figure 9-2.

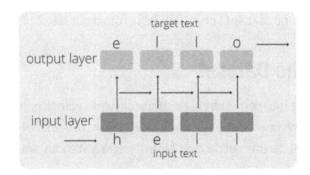

Figure 9-2. *An Example of RNN with Four-Dimensional Input and Output Layers. Note the Lag Between Input and Output Characters*

Finally, we shuffle our dataset and split into 64 sentence batches with the following lines:

```
BUFFER_SIZE = 10000 # TF shuffles the data only within buffers
BATCH_SIZE = 64 # Batch size

dataset = dataset.shuffle(BUFFER_SIZE).batch(BATCH_SIZE, drop_
remainder=True)
print(dataset)
```

Output:
```
<BatchDataset shapes: ((64, 100), (64, 100)), types: (tf.int64,
tf.int64)
```

Building the Model

Our data is ready to be fed into our model pipeline. Let's create our model. We would like to train our model and then make new predictions. What is important about this is that our training pipeline will feed 64 sentences at each batch. Therefore, we need to build our model in a way to accept 64 input sentences at a time. However, after we trained our model, we would like to input single sentences to generate new tasks. So, we need different batch sizes for pre-training and post-training models. To achieve this, we need to create a function, which allows us to reproduce models for different batch sizes. The following code does this:

```
def build_model(vocab_size, embedding_dim, rnn_units, batch_size):

  model = tf.keras.Sequential([

    tf.keras.layers.Embedding(
            vocab_size,
            embedding_dim,
            batch_input_shape=[batch_size, None]),

    tf.keras.layers.GRU(
            rnn_units,
            return_sequences=True,
            stateful=True,
            recurrent_initializer='glorot_uniform'),

    tf.keras.layers.Dense(vocab_size)

  ])
  return model
```

There are three layers in our model:

- **An Embedding Layer**: This layer serves as the input layer, accepting input values (in number format) and convert them into vectors.

- **A GRU Layer**: An RNN layer filled with 1024 gradient descent units

- **A Dense Layer**: To output the result, with `vocab_size` outputs.

Now we can create our model for training, with the following code:

```
model = build_model(
    vocab_size = len(vocab), # no. of unique characters
    embedding_dim=embedding_dim, # 256
    rnn_units=rnn_units, # 1024
    batch_size=BATCH_SIZE)  # 64 for the training
```

Here is the summary of our model in Figure 9-3.

```
Model: "sequential"
```

Layer (type)	Output Shape	Param #
embedding (Embedding)	(64, None, 256)	16640
gru (GRU)	(64, None, 1024)	3938304
dense (Dense)	(64, None, 65)	66625

```
Total params: 4,021,569
Trainable params: 4,021,569
Non-trainable params: 0
```

Figure 9-3. *The Summary View of the Training Model. Note the 64 in the Output Shapes, Which Must Be 1 for Individual Predictions After Training*

Compiling and Training the Model

To compile our model, we need to configure our optimizer and loss function. For this task, we select "Adam" as our optimizer and sparse categorical crossentropy function as our loss function.

Since our output is always one of the 65 characters, this is a multiclass categorization problem. Therefore, we have to choose a categorical crossentropy function. However, in this example, we select a variant of categorical crossentropy: sparse categorical crossentropy. The reason that we are using sparse categorical crossentropy is that even though they use the same loss function, their output formats are different. Remember we vectorized our text as integers (e.g., [0], [2], [1]), not in one-hot encoded format (e.g., [0,0,0], [0,1,], [1,0,0]). To be able to output integers, we must use a sparse categorical crossentropy function.

To be able to set our customized loss function, let's create a basic Python function containing sparse categorical crossentropy loss:

```
def loss(labels, logits):
  return tf.keras.losses.sparse_categorical_crossentropy(
labels, logits, from_logits=True)
```

Now we can set our loss function and optimizer with the following code:

```
model.compile(optimizer='adam', loss=loss)
```

To able to load our weights and save our training performance, we need to set and configure a checkpoint directory with the following code:

```
# Directory where the checkpoints will be saved
checkpoint_dir = './training_checkpoints'

# Name of the checkpoint files
checkpoint_prefix = os.path.join(checkpoint_dir, "ckpt_
{epoch}")
```

```
checkpoint_callback=tf.keras.callbacks.ModelCheckpoint(
    filepath=checkpoint_prefix,
    save_weights_only=True)
```

Our model and checkpoint directory are configured. We will train our model for 30 epochs and save the training history to a variable called history, with the following code:

```
EPOCHS = 30
history = model.fit(dataset, epochs=EPOCHS,
callbacks=[checkpoint_callback])
```

While training the model we get the following output shown in Figure 9-4:

```
Epoch 23/30
172/172 [==============================] - 22s 127ms/step - loss: 0.8086
Epoch 24/30
172/172 [==============================] - 22s 127ms/step - loss: 0.7845
Epoch 25/30
172/172 [==============================] - 22s 127ms/step - loss: 0.7628
Epoch 26/30
172/172 [==============================] - 22s 127ms/step - loss: 0.7456
Epoch 27/30
172/172 [==============================] - 22s 127ms/step - loss: 0.7304
Epoch 28/30
172/172 [==============================] - 22s 127ms/step - loss: 0.7141
Epoch 29/30
172/172 [==============================] - 22s 128ms/step - loss: 0.7034
Epoch 30/30
172/172 [==============================] - 22s 127ms/step - loss: 0.6925
```

Figure 9-4. *The Last Eight Epochs of the Model Training*

Thanks to the simplicity of the model and the way we encode our model, our training does not take too long (around 3–4 minutes). Now we can use the saved weights and build a custom model that accepts single input to generate text.

Generating Text with the Trained Model

To be able to view the location of our latest checkpoint, we need to run the following code:

```
tf.train.latest_checkpoint(checkpoint_dir)
```
Output:
```
./training_checkpoints/ckpt_30
```

Now we can use the custom build_model() function we created earlier to build a new model with batch_size=1, load weights using the weights saved in the latest_checkpoint, and use the build() function to build the model based on input shapes received (i.e., [1, None]). We can achieve all of these and summarize() the information on our new model with the following code:

```
model = build_model(vocab_size, embedding_dim, rnn_units,
batch_size=1)
model.load_weights(tf.train.latest_checkpoint(checkpoint_dir))
model.build(tf.TensorShape([1, None]))
model.summary()
```

The output is shown in Figure 9-5:

Output:

```
Model: "sequential_1"

Layer (type)                 Output Shape              Param #
=================================================================
embedding_1 (Embedding)      (1, None, 256)            16640

gru_1 (GRU)                  (1, None, 1024)           3938304

dense_1 (Dense)              (1, None, 65)             66625
=================================================================
Total params: 4,021,569
Trainable params: 4,021,569
Non-trainable params: 0
```

Figure 9-5. *The Summary View of the Newly Created Model. Now It Accepts Single Inputs*

Our model is ready to make predictions, and all we need is a custom function to prepare our input for the model. We have to set the following:

- The number of characters to generate

- Vectorizing the input (from string to numbers)

- An empty variable to store the result

- A temperature value to manually adjust variability of the predictions

- Devectorizing the output and also feeding the output to the model again for the next prediction

- Joining all the generated characters to have a final string

The following custom function does all of these:

```
def generate_text(model, num_generate, temperature, start_
string):
  input_eval = [char2idx[s] for s in start_string] # string to
                                                    numbers
                                                    (vectorizing)
  input_eval = tf.expand_dims(input_eval, 0) # dimension
                                             expansion
  text_generated = [] # Empty string to store our results
  model.reset_states() # Clears the hidden states in the RNN

  for i in range(num_generate): #Run a loop for number of
                                characters to generate
    predictions = model(input_eval) # prediction for single
                                    character
    predictions = tf.squeeze(predictions, 0) # remove the batch
                                             dimension
```

```
# using a categorical distribution to predict the character
  returned by the model
# higher temperature increases the probability of selecting
  a less likely character
# lower --> more predictable
predictions = predictions / temperature
predicted_id = tf.random.categorical(predictions, num_
samples=1)[-1,0].numpy()

# The predicted character as the next input to the model
# along with the previous hidden state
# So the model makes the next prediction based on the
  previous character
input_eval = tf.expand_dims([predicted_id], 0)
# Also devectorize the number and add to the generated text
text_generated.append(idx2char[predicted_id])

 return (start_string + ''.join(text_generated))
```

It returns our final prediction value, and we can easily generate a text using the following line:

```
generated_text = generate_text(
                    model,
                    num_generate=500,
                    temperature=1,
                    start_string=u"ROMEO")
```

And we can print it out with the built-in print function:

```
print(generated_text)
```

Output:
ROMEO:

Third Servingman:
This attemptue never long to smile
under garlands grass and enterhoand of death.

GREMIO:
Have I not fought for such a joy? can come to Spilet O, thy
husband!
Go, sirs, confusion's cut off? princely Noboth, my any thing
thee;
Whereto we will kiss thy lips.

ANTIGONUS:
It is your office: you have ta'en her relatants so many friends
as they
or no man upon the market-play with thee!

GRUMIO:
First, know, my lord.

KING RICHARD II:
Then why.

CORIOLANUS:
How like a tinker? Was e

As you can see, our model is capable of generating text in any length.
Please note this: Our model uses characters, so the miracle of the model is
that it learned to create meaningful words from characters. So, do not think
that it adds a bunch of unrelated words together. It goes over thousands
of words and learns the relationship between different characters and
how they are used to create meaningful words. Then it replicates this and
returns us sentences with meaningful words.

Please play around with temperature to see how you can change the output from more proper words to more distorted words. A higher temperature value would increase the chances of our function to choose less likely characters. When we add them all up, we would have less meaningful results. A low temperature, on the other hand, would cause the function to generate text that is simpler and more of a copy of the original corpus.

Conclusion

In this chapter, we covered natural language processing, a subfield of artificial intelligence, which deals with text data. We covered the major methods and techniques used in NLP studies. We also briefly visited the timeline of NLP. We finally conducted a case study, where we use recurrent neural networks to generate Shakespeare-like text.

In the next chapter, we will cover the recommender systems, which are the backbone of the many services provided by the large tech companies we know today.

CHAPTER 10

Recommender Systems

Recommender systems (RSs) are powerful information filtering systems that rank items and recommend them to a user based on the preferences of the user and the features of the items. These recommendations can vary from which movies to watch to what products to purchase, from which songs to listen to which services to receive. The goal of recommender systems is to suggest the right items to the user to build a trust relationship to achieve long-term business objectives. Most of the large tech companies such as Amazon, Netflix, Spotify, YouTube, and Google benefit from recommender systems to a great extent; see Figure 10-1 for Amazon example.

Figure 10-1. *A Recommender System for Gift Ideas on amazon.com*

© Orhan Gazi Yalçın 2021
O. G. Yalçın, *Applied Neural Networks with TensorFlow 2*,
https://doi.org/10.1007/978-1-4842-6513-0_10

Let's take a look at the popular approaches to recommender systems in the next section.

Popular Approaches

There are several approaches to create a powerful recommender system, but the two most popular approaches which are widely used are (i) collaborative filtering and (ii) content-based filtering. In this section, we will briefly cover these filtering approaches.

Collaborative Filtering

Collaborative filtering is a recommendation approach based on filtering out items that a user might prefer on the basis of the reactions of users with similar characteristics. It is based on grouping users into smaller sets of groups with similar preferences and recommending them the items that the other members of the group are satisfied with.

The primary assumption of the collaborative filtering is that the users who have agreed in the past tend to agree in the future. Therefore, pure collaborative filtering systems only need data on the historical preferences of the users on a given set of items. Figure 10-2 shows a visual explanation of the Collaborative Filtering approach.

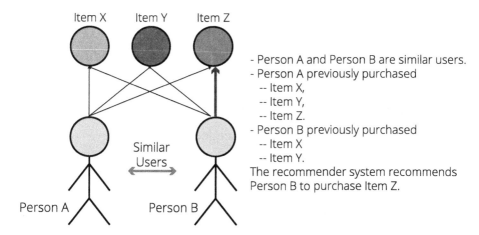

Figure 10-2. *A Depiction of Collaborative Recommender Systems*

Collaborative Filtering Sub-approaches

There are also sub-approaches within the collaborative filtering approach. Collaborative filtering can be (i) memory based or (ii) model based. The memory-based approach is based on finding similar users using a selected measure (e.g., cosine similarity or Pearson correlation) and taking a weighted average of ratings. Although it is easy to build and more interpretable, it does not perform well when the data is limited. On the other hand, the model-based approach utilizes machine learning to predict expected user ratings of unrated items. Although this approach hinders the interpretability of the model, it is much more effective when the available data is limited.

Data Collection

Since collaborative filtering is based on users' historical data, one of the essential steps of recommender system development with a collaborative approach is to collect data about the users' feedbacks and preferences. This data can be explicit feedback or implicit behavior of the user.

217

Explicit Data Collection

Explicit data collection comprises of all the data that the user directly provides to the system. This includes

- A user's rate on an item on a sliding scale

- A user's item ranking inside a collection from most favorite to least favorite

- A user's selection between two or more items

- A user's list of favorite items

Implicit Data Collection

Implicit data collection is based on a user's observable behaviors. These observations can be made within the system as well outside of the systems with tools such as cookies and third-party solutions. Implicit data includes

- A user's viewed items list

- Record of the items that a user purchased online

- The websites that a user visited

- A user's social network engagements

Issues With Regard to Collaborative Filtering

Even though collaborative filtering works very well, there are three common issues that a recommender system might experience:

- Cold start

- Scalability

- Sparsity

Cold Start

When a recommender system is first deployed, it is very common that the size of the available data about users and items are minimal. In addition, even when the recommender system matures, sufficient information on the newly added user or product is probably much less than the desired amount, which is crucial to make valuable recommendations. Therefore, when there is not enough information, recommender systems often fail to provide a useful recommendation, which is referred to as the "cold start" problem.

Scalability

Another issue with regard to recommender systems based on collaborative filtering is the scalability. Especially when the memory-based approach is adopted for systems with millions of users, calculating the similarity measures might become a very time-consuming and resource-intensive task.

Sparsity

Finally, collecting sufficient information regarding items might be another issue to build successful recommender systems. This is due to the low percentage of feedbacks based on the items watched, sold, or listened to. Therefore, the low level of the feedback ratio might reduce the significance of the results and provide an incorrect ranking of items.

Content-Based Filtering (Personality-Based Approach)

Content-based filtering is another popular approach to recommender systems. Content refers to the content or attributes of the items that the user engages with. In the content-based filtering approach, items are categorized, and based on the user's limited feedback, the system recommends new items belonging to the categories the user likes.

For example, when you give positive ratings to action movies and negative ratings to children movies, the recommender system with the content-based filtering would recommend you another action movie.

For content-based filtering, both items and users are tagged with keywords to categorize them. Items are tagged based on their attributes, whereas to tag users, a dedicated model is designed to create user profiles based on their interaction with the recommender system. A vector space representation algorithm (e.g., tf-idf) is used to abstract the features of the items. Then, the system makes recommendations based on the algorithm.

In recent years, the recommendation systems that are solely based on content-based filtering have lost its popularity. More often than not, content-based filtering is used with other filtering methods to create hybrid models.

Other Recommender System Approaches

Apart from collaborative and content-based recommender systems, there are other kinds of recommender systems that are increasingly used.

- **Multi-criteria Recommender Systems**: These recommender systems use more than a single criterion to make a recommendation. Generally speaking, recommendation systems collect a single preference rating for an item. But a more complex user rating system can help to create a more accurate and advanced recommending system. For instance, in a movie recommendation system, instead of collecting an overall rating for a given movie, collecting ratings for specific movie aspects (e.g., acting, visual effect, cast members) can improve the recommendation performance.

- **Risk-Aware Recommender Systems**: Recommender systems with integrated risk measures are called risk-aware recommender systems. For example, the frequency (e.g., 30 times/day) and timing (e.g., during business hours) of the recommendations might affect the experience of the user, and these recommender systems take these features into account to enhance the user experience.

- **Mobile Recommender Systems**: Mobile recommender systems take advantage of the data collected by mobile devices. These recommender systems often operate in real time with momentary updates based on the changing status of the user (e.g., the location of the user).

- **Hybrid Recommender Systems**: Hybrid recommender systems combine multiple approaches such as content-based filtering, collaborative filtering, and risk assessment. They choose from, mix, or weight the outputs of each approach and deliver a final recommendation output.

Please note that the preceding list is a non-exhaustive list that grows with the advancements in the computer and data sciences.

Case Study I Deep Collaborative Filtering with MovieLens Dataset

We will build a custom neural network using Model Subclassing to implement collaborative filtering. Remember that the primary assumption of the collaborative filtering is that the users who have agreed in the past tend to agree in the future. Therefore, pure collaborative filtering systems only need the historical preferences of the users on a set of items.

MovieLens Dataset

In this case study, we use a popular movie rating dataset, MovieLens, which is designed and maintained by GroupLens. GroupLens is a research lab in the Department of Computer Science and Engineering at the University of Minnesota, and they maintain a number of datasets on their web page at `https://grouplens.org/datasets/movielens/`. On this page, you may access a number of datasets with different numbers of observations.

We prefer rather a small dataset: MovieLens Latest Small Dataset consisting of 100,000 ratings and 3,600 tag applications applied to 9,000 movies by 600 users. The approximate size of the dataset is only 1 MB, which makes our network training process very quick. The dataset is available at `http://files.grouplens.org/datasets/movielens/ml-latest-small.zip`.

During the case study, we will dive into the meaning of the columns (namely, `userId`, `movieId`, `rating`, `timestamp`) of our dataset. Let's start with the initial imports

Initial Imports

There are six initial imports we need for this case study, and they are imported for the following functionalities:

- **TensorFlow**: To build and train our model and to make predictions

- **ZipFile**: To unzip the MovieLens dataset, which is saved as a zip file

- **Pandas**: To create DataFrames and conduct basic data processing tasks

- **NumPy**: To generate NumPy arrays and conduct data processing tasks

- **train_test_split from scikit-learn**: To make a train and test split operation

- **Embedding from TensorFlow**: To import the Embedding layer from TensorFlow

- **get_file from TensorFlow**: To download the dataset from an external URL

The following lines import all the relevant libraries and functions:

```
import tensorflow as tf
from zipfile import ZipFile
import pandas as pd
import numpy as np
from sklearn.model_selection import train_test_split
from tensorflow.keras.layers import Embedding
from tensorflow.keras.utils import get_file
```

Loading the Data

Now that we completed our initial imports, we can focus on data processing and model building. We will download and load our data from the official releaser's website, GroupLens.org. Then, we will use the get_file() function from TensorFlow to download the dataset, with the following code:

```
URL = "http://files.grouplens.org/datasets/movielens/ml-latest-small.zip"
movielens_path = get_file("movielens.zip", URL, extract=True)
```

Colab will temporarily download and save the zip file containing multiple CSV files. To be able to open one of these CSV files, we need the ZipFile() function, which works as follows:

```
with ZipFile(movielens_path) as z:
  with z.open("ml-latest-small/ratings.csv") as f:
    df = pd.read_csv(f)
```

With the preceding code, we save the ratings table as a Pandas DataFrame, which is shown in Figure 10-3.

	userId	movieId	rating	timestamp
0	1	1	4.0	964982703
1	1	3	4.0	964981247
2	1	6	4.0	964982224
3	1	47	5.0	964983815
4	1	50	5.0	964982931

Figure 10-3. *The First Five Rows of the Rating Dataset*

Ratings DataFrame has four columns:

- **userId**: An ID number for each user

- **movieId**: An ID number for each movie

- **rating**: The rating for the movie given by a particular user

- **timestamp**: Shows when the movie was rated by the user

Now that we know our dataset, it is time to process our columns and prepare them for the deep learning model.

Processing the Data

In our MovieLens dataset, the user IDs start from 1, and the movie IDs are not consecutive. This is not very healthy for computational efficiency during the training. Therefore, we will give them new ID numbers, which can be mapped back to their originals later.

Processing User IDs

We first need to enumerate the unique user IDs and create a dictionary from the enumerated user IDs. Then, we also create a reverse dictionary (keys and values are reversed) with these enumerated IDs. Then, we create a new column for the new user IDs, named user. Finally, we save the unique user count as num_users, with the following code:

```
user_ids = df["userId"].unique().tolist()
user2user_encoded = {x: i for i, x in enumerate(user_ids)}
user_encoded2user = {i: x for i, x in enumerate(user_ids)}
df["user"] = df["userId"].map(user2user_encoded)
num_users = len(user_encoded2user)
```

Processing Movie IDs

For the movie IDs, we also follow a similar path with the user IDs. This step is even more important for movie IDs, since these IDs are not given consecutively in our dataset. The following code process the movie IDs, create a new column with new IDs, and save the unique movie count as num_movies:

```
movie_ids = df["movieId"].unique().tolist()
movie2movie_encoded = {x: i for i, x in enumerate(movie_ids)}
movie_encoded2movie = {i: x for i, x in enumerate(movie_ids)}
df["movie"] = df["movieId"].map(movie2movie_encoded)
num_movies = len(movie_encoded2movie)
```

Now we can view how many users and movies are there in the dataset with the following code:

```
print("Number of users: ", num_users,
      "\nNumber of Movies: ", num_movies)
```
Output:
```
Number of users:  610
Number of Movies:  9724
```

Processing the Ratings

For the ratings, all we should do is to normalize them for computational efficiency and the reliability of the model. We need to detect the min and max ratings and then apply a lambda function for Minmax normalization. The following code successfully does that:

```
min, max  = df["rating"].min(), df["rating"].max()
df["rating"] = df["rating"].apply(lambda x:(x-min)/(max-min))
```

Let's take a final look at our processed df DataFrame with Figure 10-4:

	userId	movieId	rating	timestamp	user	movie
0	1	1	0.777778	964982703	0	0
1	1	3	0.777778	964981247	0	1
2	1	6	0.777778	964982224	0	2
3	1	47	1.000000	964983815	0	3
4	1	50	1.000000	964982931	0	4

Figure 10-4. *The First Five Rows of the Processed Rating Dataset*

Splitting the Dataset

Since this is a supervised learning task, we need to split our data as (i) features (Xs) and labels (Y) and as (ii) training and validation sets.

For the features and labels split, we can just choose the columns and save it as new variables, as shown here:

```
X = df[["user", "movie"]].values
y = df["rating"].values
```

New user and movie columns are our features, which we will use to predict user ratings for an unseen movie.

For the train and validation split, we can use train_test_split() function from scikit-learn, which splits and shuffles our dataset. The following code is enough to split our dataset:

```
(x_train, x_val, y_train, y_val) = train_test_split(
        X, y,
        test_size=0.1,
        random_state=42)
```

Let's take a look at the shape of our four new datasets:

```
print("Shape of the x_train: ", x_train.shape)
print("Shape of the y_train: ", y_train.shape)
print("Shape of the x_val: ", x_val.shape)
print("Shape of the x_val: ", y_val.shape)
```
Output:
```
Shape of the x_train:  (90752, 2)
Shape of the y_train:  (90752,)
Shape of the x_val:  (10084, 2)
Shape of the x_val:  (10084,)
```

Building the Model

In TensorFlow, apart from Sequential API and Functional API, there is a third option to build models: Model Subclassing. In Model Subclassing, we are free to implement everything from scratch. Model Subclassing is fully customizable and enables us to implement our own custom model. It is a very powerful method since we can build any type of model. However, it requires a basic level of object-oriented programming knowledge. Our custom class would subclass the `tf.keras.Model` object. It also requires declaring several variables and functions. However, it is nothing to be afraid of. To build a model, we simply need to complete the following tasks:

- Create a class extending `keras.Model` object.

- Create an __init__ function to declare seven variables that we use in our model:

  - `embedding_size`

  - `num_users`

  - `user_embedding`

  - `user_bias`

  - `num_movies`

  - `movie_embedding`

  - `movie_bias`

- Create a call function to tell the model how to process the inputs using the initialized variables with __init__ function.

- Return the output in the end after a Sigmoid activation layer.

The following code does all of them (please note that most of the code is comment):

```
class RecommenderNet(tf.keras.Model):
    # __init function is to initialize the values of
    # instance members for the new object
    def __init__(self, num_users, num_movies, embedding_size,
    **kwargs):
        super(RecommenderNet, self).__init__(**kwargs)
        # Variable for embedding size
        self.embedding_size = embedding_size

        # Variables for user count, and related weights and biases
        self.num_users = num_users
        self.user_embedding = Embedding(
            num_users,
            embedding_size,
            embeddings_initializer="he_normal",
            embeddings_regularizer=tf.keras.regularizers.
            l2(1e-6),
        )
        self.user_bias = Embedding(num_users, 1)

        # Variables for movie count, and related weights and
        biases
        self.num_movies = num_movies
        self.movie_embedding = Embedding(
            num_movies,
            embedding_size,
            embeddings_initializer="he_normal",
            embeddings_regularizer=tf.keras.regularizers.
            l2(1e-6),
        )
```

```
        self.movie_bias = Embedding(num_movies, 1)

    def call(self, inputs):
        # call function is for the dot products
        # of user and movie vectors
        # It also accepts the inputs, feeds them into the
        layers,
        # and feed into the final sigmoid layer

        # User vector and bias values with input values
        user_vector = self.user_embedding(inputs[:, 0])
        user_bias = self.user_bias(inputs[:, 0])

        # Movie vector and bias values with input values
        movie_vector = self.movie_embedding(inputs[:, 1])
        movie_bias = self.movie_bias(inputs[:, 1])
        # tf.tensordot calculcates the dot product
        dot_user_movie = tf.tensordot(user_vector, movie_
        vector, 2)
        # Add all the components (including bias)
        x = dot_user_movie + user_bias + movie_bias

        # The sigmoid activation forces the rating to between 0
        and 1
        return tf.nn.sigmoid(x)
```

After declaring the RecommenderNet class, we can create an instance of this custom class to build our custom RecommenderNet model:

```
model = RecommenderNet(num_users, num_movies, embedding_
size=50)
```

Compile and Train the Model

After creating our model, we can configure it. Since we are working on to predict the rating of an unseen movie, it is more of a regression task. Therefore, using the mean squared error (MSE) measure – instead of a crossentropy measure – would be a better choice. In addition, we also choose Adam optimizer as our optimizer. The following code does all of them:

```
model.compile(
    loss='mse',
    optimizer=tf.keras.optimizers.Adam(lr=0.001)
)
```

We will train our custom model for 5 epochs with the following code:

```
history = model.fit(
    x=x_train,
    y=y_train,
    batch_size=64,
    epochs=5,
    verbose=1,
    validation_data=(x_val, y_val),
)
```

Figure 10-5 shows the MSE loss values at each epoch.

```
Epoch 1/5
1418/1418 [==============================] - 4s 3ms/step - loss: 0.0540 - val_loss: 0.0469
Epoch 2/5
1418/1418 [==============================] - 4s 3ms/step - loss: 0.0438 - val_loss: 0.0460
Epoch 3/5
1418/1418 [==============================] - 4s 3ms/step - loss: 0.0417 - val_loss: 0.0436
Epoch 4/5
1418/1418 [==============================] - 5s 3ms/step - loss: 0.0412 - val_loss: 0.0442
Epoch 5/5
1418/1418 [==============================] - 5s 3ms/step - loss: 0.0406 - val_loss: 0.0446
```

Figure 10-5. *The Epoch Stats During Our Custom Model Training*

Make Recommendations

Now our model is trained and ready to make recommendations with collaborative filtering. We can randomly pick a user ID with the following code:

```
user_id = df.userId.sample(1).iloc[0]
print("The selected user ID is: ", user_id)
```

Output: The selected user ID is: 414

Next step is to filter out the movies that the user watched before. The following code makes a list of the movies that the user has not seen before:

```
movies_watched = df[df.userId == user_id]
not_watched = df[~df['movieId'].isin(movies_watched.movieId.
values)]['movieId'].unique()
not_watched = [[movie2movie_encoded.get(x)] for x in not_
watched]
print('The number of movies the user has not seen before: ',
len(not_watched))
```

Output: The number of movies the user has not seen before is 7026

With the following code, we get the user's new ID number that we gave them during the initial data processing step, then create a NumPy array with np.hstack() function, and use the model.predict() function to generate the predicted movie ratings:

```
user_encoder = user2user_encoded.get(user_id)
user_movie_array = np.hstack(
        ([[user_encoder]] * len(not_watched), not_watched )
        )
ratings = model.predict(user_movie_array).flatten()
```

The preceding code gives us a NumPy array, which includes a normalized rating value for all the movies. But we don't need all of them. We only need the top 10 movies with the highest ratings. In addition, we need their ID numbers so that we can map them to understand which titles they have.

NumPy `argsort()` function sorts all the items and returns their indices (IDs). Finally, we need to reverse them since it works in ascending order. The following code completes all these tasks:

```
top10_indices = ratings.argsort()[-10:][::-1]
```

The following code converts our assigned movie IDs to their original movie IDs given in the dataset:

```
recommended_movie_ids = [
    movie_encoded2movie.get(not_watched[x][0]) for x in top10_
indices
]
```

Now we have the original IDs of the top 10 movies. But we cannot just show users movie IDs. Instead, we would want to show them movie titles with their genre information. Therefore, we need to make use of another CSV file in our zip file: movies.csv. The following code will load the dataset and create a Pandas DataFrame, named movie_df (see Figure 10-6 for the output):

```
# Create a DataFrame from Movies.csv file
with ZipFile(movielens_path) as z:
    with z.open("ml-latest-small/movies.csv") as f:
        movie_df = pd.read_csv(f)
movie_df.head(2)
```

	movieId	title	genres
0	1	Toy Story (1995)	Adventure|Animation|Children|Comedy|Fantasy
1	2	Jumanji (1995)	Adventure|Children|Fantasy

Figure 10-6. *The First Two Rows of the Movies Dataset*

Let's check the movies that the user already watched and gave a high rating by filtering their top 10 movies watched:

```
top_movies_user = (
    movies_watched.sort_values(by="rating", ascending=False)
    .head(10)
    .movieId.values
)
movie_df_rows = movie_df[movie_df["movieId"].isin(top_movies_
user)]
```

We can view them by running the following code, as shown in Figure 10-7:

```
print("Movies with high ratings from user")
movie_df_rows[['title','genres']]
```

Movies with high ratings from the user

	title	genres
602	Dr. Strangelove or: How I Learned to Stop Worr...	Comedy|War
692	Some Like It Hot (1959)	Comedy|Crime
694	Casablanca (1942)	Drama|Romance
698	Roman Holiday (1953)	Comedy|Drama|Romance
705	Citizen Kane (1941)	Drama|Mystery
706	2001: A Space Odyssey (1968)	Adventure|Drama|Sci-Fi
733	It's a Wonderful Life (1946)	Children|Drama|Fantasy|Romance
961	Great Escape, The (1963)	Action|Adventure|Drama|War
1550	Peter Pan (1953)	Animation|Children|Fantasy|Musical
3240	Princess and the Warrior, The (Krieger und die...	Drama|Romance

Figure 10-7. *List of the Movies with High Ratings from the User*

Now we can also view the top 10 movies our collaborative filtering model would recommend the user with the following code and in Figure 10-8.

```
recommended_movies = movie_df[movie_df["movieId"].
isin(recommended_movie_ids)]
print("Top 10 movie recommendations")
recommended_movies[['title','genres']]
```

Top 10 movie recommendations

	title	genres
680	Philadelphia Story, The (1940)	Comedy|Drama|Romance
704	Sunset Blvd. (a.k.a. Sunset Boulevard) (1950)	Drama|Film-Noir|Romance
711	Notorious (1946)	Film-Noir|Romance|Thriller
920	Psycho (1960)	Crime|Horror
930	Annie Hall (1977)	Comedy|Romance
957	Shining, The (1980)	Horror
1616	Rosemary's Baby (1968)	Drama|Horror|Thriller
1640	Strangers on a Train (1951)	Crime|Drama|Film-Noir|Thriller
1730	Life Is Beautiful (La Vita è bella) (1997)	Comedy|Drama|Romance|War
8395	Captain America: The Winter Soldier (2014)	Action|Adventure|Sci-Fi|IMAX

Figure 10-8. *The Top 10 Movie Recommendation for the User*

As you can see, most of the movies the user watched are classics, and our recommender system also recommended the user movies from the 1940s throughout to the 1970s. Besides, the genres are also similar to a great extent between watched and recommended movies.

In this case study, we successfully built a working recommender system based on a pure collaborative filtering approach. You can easily change the userId and make recommendations for other users to test the success of the model. In addition, you can use a different and, possibly, larger MovieLens dataset to increase the accuracy of the model. Try to play around the variables and test your model.

Conclusion

In this chapter, we covered recommender systems, which can be built using neural networks. We covered different approaches to recommender systems and built a recommender system using MovieLens dataset based on deep collaborative filtering. This recommender system was capable of suggesting the unseen movies that the user most likely to enjoy.

In the next chapter, we will cover the autoencoder networks, which are mainly used for unsupervised learning tasks.

CHAPTER 11

Autoencoders

In the previous chapters, we covered feedforward NNs, CNNs, and RNNs. These networks are predominantly used for supervised learning tasks. In this chapter, we focus on autoencoders (see Figure 11-1), a neural network architecture which is mainly used for unsupervised learning tasks.

The main promise of the autoencoders is to learn an encoding structure and a decoding structure for a given set of data. Autoencoders are mainly used for dimensionality reduction, noise reduction, and several generative tasks. There are several variants of autoencoders designated for particular tasks, but first, let's dive into the architecture of autoencoders.

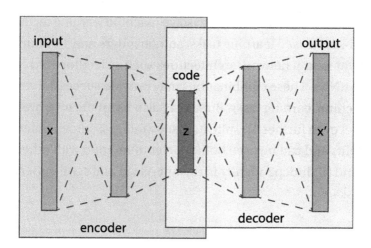

Figure 11-1. *A Rough Visualization of Autoencoder Architecture*

© Orhan Gazi Yalçın 2021
O. G. Yalçın, *Applied Neural Networks with TensorFlow 2,*
https://doi.org/10.1007/978-1-4842-6513-0_11

Advantages and Disadvantages of Autoencoders

Autoencoders are very promising neural network architectures that are regarded as powerful alternatives to other unsupervised machine learning models such as principal component analysis.

In reality, autoencoders can do everything that a PCA model does and more. A pure linear autoencoder would give the same results with PCA. But, in a nonlinear feature extraction problem, an autoencoder can do much more than a PCA model. In most cases, these problems have a nonlinear nature, and therefore, they are sure to outperform PCA models.

But not everything is black and white. Just like other neural network architectures, autoencoders require a lot of data and computing power compared to a PCA model. In addition, a poorly structured training dataset used in autoencoder training can even further obscure the features that we are trying to extract because autoencoders focus on extracting all the information instead of extracting the relevant information. Therefore, poorly structured datasets can be harmful to solve machine learning the task.

In semi-supervised learning tasks, autoencoders may be coupled with different neural network architectures such as feedforward NNs, CNNs, and RNNs. These combinations may provide successful results in several machine learning tasks. But it may also harm the interpretability of the model even further. Despite its disadvantages, autoencoders offer many benefits and can be used both (i) in combination with other neural networks and (ii) independently in unsupervised and semi-supervised learning tasks.

Autoencoder Architecture

Autoencoders were first introduced in the 1980s by Hinton and the PDP group. The main purpose of this proposal was to address the unsupervised backpropagation problem (a.k.a. "backpropagation without a teacher" problem).

The most important structural feature of an autoencoder network is its ability to encode an input, only to decode to its original form. Therefore, the input and output ends of an autoencoder are almost exclusively fed with the same data. This would eliminate the necessity of label data for supervision. Hence, there is an encoder network and a decoder network within each autoencoder network. These encoder and decoder networks are connected via a narrow latent space, as shown in Figure 11-2.

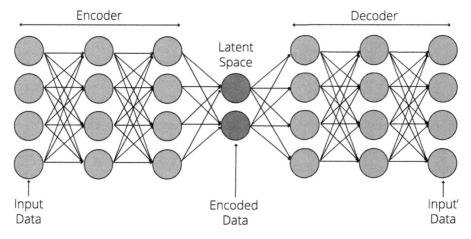

Figure 11-2. *An Example of Autoencoder Networks*

Since the main task of autoencoders is to ensure the equivalency of input and output values, autoencoder networks are forced to preserve the most relevant information within the network to reconstruct the input values in the end. This nature makes autoencoders very suitable for dimensionality reduction, feature learning, and noise reduction (i.e., denoising).

The most basic form of an autoencoder consists of three main components: (i) an input layer, (ii) a latent space layer, and (iii) an output layer. The input layer, together with the latent space, comprises the encoder network, whereas the output layer, together with the latent space, comprises the decoder network. The simple multilayer perceptron, which brings together the encoder and the decoder, is an example of the basic autoencoder, shown in Figure 11-3.

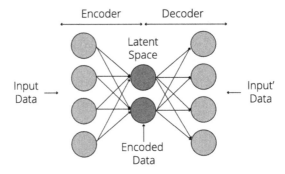

Figure 11-3. *An Example of the Basic Autoencoder Network*

The goal is to adjust weights in an optimized way to minimize the differences between the input layer and output layer values. This is achieved through the backpropagation of the error terms, similar to feedforward neural networks.

Layers Used in an Autoencoder

The layers that can be used in an autoencoder might vary based on the problem. Every autoencoder must have an encoder and a decoder network, which are connected via a layer, namely, latent space. This is the promise of the autoencoder, and you can add any type of layer inside these networks, including but not limited to, dense, convolution, pooling, LSTM, GRU layers. In fact, encoder and decoder networks can be designed as standalone feedforward, CNN, or RNN networks based on the nature of the task at hand. On the other hand, in most autoencoder applications, decoder networks are designed as the reversed version of encoder networks to ensure the convergence of the model. For example, when you build a CNN-based encoder with convolution layers, the decoder network must consist of transpose convolution layers.

Advantages of Depth

In Figure 11-3, you can see the basic version of autoencoders. But, in most real-world applications, multiple layers are inserted in encoder and decoder networks for three reasons:

- **A Better Compression Compared to Shallow Autoencoders**: Multilayer autoencoders do a better job in compressing the important information to latent space compared to shallow autoencoders.

- **Lower Cost (Error) Measures**: Generally speaking, multilayer networks are better at converging on complex functions, which reduces the cost measures such as MSE.

- **A Lower Amount of Training Data Needed**: Multilayer autoencoders can converge better than shallow autoencoders when the amount of available data is limited.

In the next section, let's take a look at the autoencoder variations.

Variations of Autoencoders

All the autoencoder types have an encoder-decoder architecture, but there are several variations of autoencoders to address specific machine learning tasks. There are three main groups: (i) undercomplete autoencoders, (ii) regularized autoencoders, and (iii) variational autoencoders (VAEs).

Undercomplete Autoencoders

Undercomplete autoencoders are the basic autoencoders, which constrains the number of neurons in latent space to have a smaller dimension than the input layer. An autoencoder with a smaller neuron count in its latent space compared to the neuron count in the input layer is called an undercomplete autoencoder.

Undercomplete autoencoders copy the input to output, and it may seem pointless. But, the useful part of the autoencoder is its latent space, and the output of the decoder is rarely used. The goal of an autoencoder is to extract features by summarizing them in the latent space located in the intersection of encoder and decoder networks.

However, in some cases, autoencoder only copies the task from the encoder to the decoder (i.e., input to output) without learning anything significant. To be able to eliminate this possibility, the capacity of the autoencoders is limited with regularization methods. These autoencoders, whose capacities are limited, comprise the family of regularized autoencoders.

Regularized Autoencoders

One of the main issues encountered in autoencoders is the tendency to make a symmetric copy of the encoder structure for the decoder. This issue damages the autoencoder's ability to derive meaningful features from the model. There are several methods to prevent autoencoders from making a copy of its encoder network for the decoder, which is crucial to capture information. The variations of regularized autoencoders are configured with specialized cost functions that encourage these autoencoders to discover meaningful features and prevent them from uselessly copying the input to the output. There are three popular variations of regularized autoencoders:

- Sparse autoencoder (SAE)

- Denoising autoencoder (DAE)

- Contractive autoencoder (CAE)

Sparse Autoencoder (SAE)

Sparse autoencoders (SAEs) are autoencoders that rely on the sparsity of the active neurons inside the latent space. Generally, the number of neurons in latent space is less than the number of neurons in input and output layers, which makes them undercomplete. On the other hand, there are autoencoders which have more neurons in the latent space than in the input layer, which are called overcomplete.

Both undercomplete and overcomplete autoencoders may fail to learn meaningful features in particular cases, and sparse autoencoders address this issue by introducing sparsity to the latent space. During the training, some of the neurons are deliberately inactivated, which forces the model to learn meaningful features from the data. Therefore, the autoencoders must respond to unique statistical features of the dataset rather than merely acting as an identity function with the sole purpose of satisfying the equation. Sparse autoencoders are generally used to extract features that are used for another task, such as classification.

Denoising Autoencoder (DAE)

Denoising autoencoders (DAEs) are special autoencoders, which are designed to minimize the error between the original input and a corrupted copy of the input by making accurate approximations. Therefore, denoising autoencoders must find ways to measure the differences between corrupted copy and the original copy. After they learned the difference between the corrupted copy and the original copy and how to eliminate this difference, they can be used to clean noisy data. For example, we can use a dataset of images with their noise-added copies to train a denoising autoencoder network. Then, this trained model can be used in the real world to clean noisy image files.

Contractive Autoencoder (CAE)

Contractive autoencoders (CAEs) are mainly used in parallel with other autoencoder types. Since they are less sensitive to small variations in the training dataset, they are very handy in dimensionality reduction and generative tasks, especially when other autoencoder types fail to learn meaningful features. This learning is achieved by adding a specific regularizer to the cost function that the optimizer algorithm tries to minimize. This specific regularizer corresponds with the Frobenius norm of the Jacobian matrix (the matrix of all the first-order partial derivatives of a function) of the encoder activations regarding the input data.

While the regularizing strategy for the contractive autoencoder is similar to sparse autoencoders, its resistance to small changes – although with different means – shows resemblances to the resistance of denoising autoencoders. As mentioned earlier, they are often used together with other autoencoders as a last resort when the other autoencoders fail to learn meaningful features.

Variational Autoencoder (VAE)

Variational autoencoders (VAEs) are mainly used for generative tasks, unlike other autoencoders, such as sparse and denoising autoencoders. Their functionality is more similar to generative adversarial networks, and they are regarded as a variant of autoencoders due to their network architecture (consisting of an encoder network and a decoder network).

For generative tasks, we need random variations from continuous functions. However, plain autoencoders do not provide continuous space. Therefore, what makes VAEs different compared to the other autoencoders is its continuous space, placed in the latent space.

Continuous space is created with two neurons, a mean and a variance neuron. These two neurons are used to get a sampled encoding, which is passed to the decoder, as shown in Figure 11-4. As encodings are generated from a distribution with the same mean and variance as those of the inputs, the decoder learns from all nearby points referred to the same latent space, which enables the model to generate similar, but not identical, outputs using the input data.

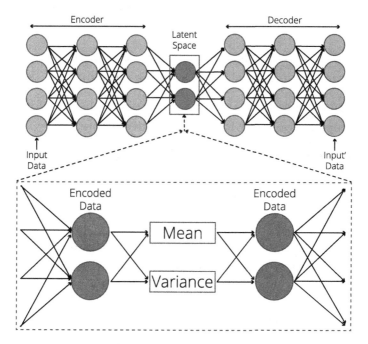

Figure 11-4. *A Visualization of Variational Autoencoders*

Use Cases of Autoencoders

Although the traditional use case of autoencoders is dimensionality reduction, as the research around autoencoders matures, new use cases for autoencoders has been observed. A non-exhaustive list of autoencoder use cases is as follows:

- **Dimensionality Reduction**: By mapping a high feature space in the input layer to the lower feature space in the latent space, autoencoders can reduce the dimensionality. A very basic autoencoder with a linear activation function would render the same result with the principal component analysis (PCA) method.

- **Noise Reduction**: Especially denoising autoencoders can successfully remove the noise in images, videos, sounds, and other types of data.

- **Image Processing**: Autoencoders may be used for image compression as well as image denoising.

- **Drug Discovery**: Variational encoders can be used for drug discovery due to their generative nature.

- **Machine Translation**: By feeding the text in the source language as input and the target language text as output, autoencoders can learn the significant features required for neural machine translation.

- Additionally, autoencoders are used in many other tasks such as information retrieval, anomaly detection, population synthesis, and popularity prediction.

Case Study I Image Denoising with Fashion MNIST

Now that we covered the conceptual part of autoencoders, we can move on to the case study. For this case study, we do our own take on one of TensorFlow's official tutorials, Intro to Autoencoders.[1]

---

[1]Intro to Autoencoders, TensorFlow, available on `www.tensorflow.org/ tutorials/generative/autoencoder`

The goal of the case study is to denoise (cleaning the noise) images. For this task, we apply our entire dataset with random noise. Then, we feed this dataset consisting of noisy images to one end of the autoencoder while feeding the clean version to the other end. After the training steps, our autoencoder learns how to clean image noise.

Fashion MNIST Dataset

In this case study, we use yet another popular dataset for the AI community: Fashion MNIST. Fashion MNIST is designed and maintained by Zalando, a European ecommerce company based in Berlin, Germany. Fashion MNIST consists of a training set of 60,000 images and a test set of 10,000 images. Each example is a 28 x 28 grayscale image, associated with a label from 10 classes. Fashion MNIST, which contains images of clothing items (as shown in Figure 11-5), is designed as an alternative dataset to MNIST dataset, which contains handwritten digits.

Initial Imports

There are seven initial imports we need for this case study, and they are imported for the following functionalities:

- **TensorFlow**: To build and train our model and to make predictions

- **Matplotlib**: To discover our dataset and visualize our results

- **NumPy**: To generate NumPy arrays and conduct data processing tasks

- **Pandas**: To create DataFrames and conduct basic data processing tasks

- fashion_mnist **from TensorFlow**: To directly load the Fashion MNIST dataset to Colab notebook

- train_test_split **from scikit-learn**: To make a train and test split operation

- Conv2DTranspose, Conv2D, **and** Input **layers from TensorFlow**: To build an autoencoder model with these layers

The following lines import all the relevant libraries and methods:

```
import tensorflow as tf
import matplotlib.pyplot as plt
import numpy as np
import pandas as pd

from tensorflow.keras.datasets import fashion_mnist
from sklearn.model_selection import train_test_split
from tensorflow.keras.layers import Conv2DTranspose, Conv2D,
Input
```

Loading and Processing the Data

After the initial imports, we can easily download and load the Fashion MNIST dataset with the following code:

```
# We don't need y_train and y_test
(x_train, _), (x_test, _) = fashion_mnist.load_data()
print('Max value in the x_train is', x_train[0].max())
print('Min value in the x_train is', x_train[0].min())
```
Output:
```
Max value in the x_train is 255
Min value in the x_train is 0
```

Now we have two datasets containing arrays that represent the pixel values of images. Note that we will not use the labels, so we did not even save y values.

Let's take a sample of the dataset and plot the images with the following Matplotlib code:

```
fig, axs = plt.subplots(5, 10)
plt.figure(figsize=(5, 10))
fig.tight_layout(pad=-1)
a = 0
for i in range(5):
  for j in range(10):
    axs[i, j].imshow(tf.squeeze(x_test[a]))
    axs[i, j].xaxis.set_visible(False)
    axs[i, j].yaxis.set_visible(False)
    a = a + 1
    plt.gray()
```

Figure 11-5 shows the output, a grid of selected apparel items:

Output:

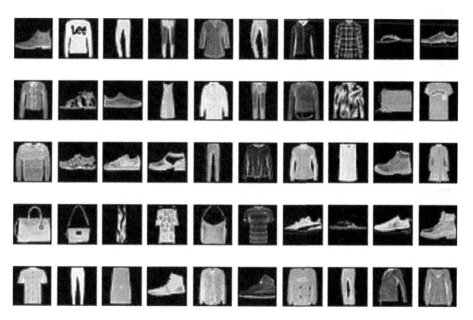

Figure 11-5. *Examples from Fashion MNIST Dataset*

For computational efficiency and model reliability, we have to apply Minmax normalization to our image data, limiting the value range between 0 and 1. Since our data is in RGB format, our minimum value is 0 and maximum value is 255, and we can conduct the Minmax normalization operation with the following lines:

```
x_train = x_train.astype('float32') / 255.
x_test = x_test.astype('float32') / 255.
```

We also have to reshape our NumPy array as the current shape of the datasets is (60000, 28, 28) and (10000, 28, 28). We just need to add a fourth dimension with a single value (*e.g., from (60000, 28, 28) to (60000, 28, 28, 1)*). The fourth dimension acts pretty much as a proof that our data is in grayscale format with a single value representing color information ranging from white to black. If we'd have colored images, then we would need three values in our fourth dimension. But all we need is a fourth dimension containing a single value since we use grayscale images. The following lines do this:

```
x_train = x_train[..., tf.newaxis]
x_test = x_test[..., tf.newaxis]
```

Let's take a look at the shape of our NumPy arrays with the following lines:

```
print(x_train.shape)
print(x_test.shape)
```
Output:
```
(60000, 28, 28, 1)
(10000, 28, 28, 1)
```

Adding Noise to Images

Remember, our goal is to create a denoising autoencoder. For this task, we need clean and noisy copies of the image files. The autoencoder's task is to adjust its weights to replicate the noising process and become able to denoise noisy images as well. In other words, we deliberately add random noise to our images to distort them so that our autoencoder may learn how they became noisy and how they can be denoised. Therefore, we need to add noise to our existing images.

We add a randomly generated value to each array item by using `tf.random.normal` method. Then, we multiply the random value with a `noise_factor`, which you can play around with. The following code adds noise to images:

```
noise_factor = 0.6
x_train_noisy = x_train + noise_factor * tf.random.
normal(shape=x_train.shape)
x_test_noisy = x_test + noise_factor * tf.random.
normal(shape=x_test.shape)
```

We also need to make sure that our array item values are within the range of 0 to 1. For this, we may use `tf.clip_by_value` method. `clip_by_value` is a TensorFlow method which clips the values outside of the Min-Max range and replace them with the designated min or max value. The following code clips the values out of range:

```
x_train_noisy = tf.clip_by_value(x_train_noisy, clip_value_
min=0., clip_value_max=1.)
x_test_noisy = tf.clip_by_value(x_test_noisy, clip_value_
min=0., clip_value_max=1.)
```

Now that we have our noisy and clean images, let's see the effect of our random noise with the following code:

```
n = 5
plt.figure(figsize=(20, 8))
for i in range(n):
    ax = plt.subplot(2, n, i + 1)
    plt.title("original", size=20)
    plt.imshow(tf.squeeze(x_test[i]))
    plt.gray()

    bx = plt.subplot(2, n, n+ i + 1)
    plt.title("original + noise", size=20)
    plt.imshow(tf.squeeze(x_test_noisy[i]))
    plt.gray()
plt.show()
```

Figure 11-6 shows the original images with their noisy versions:

Output:

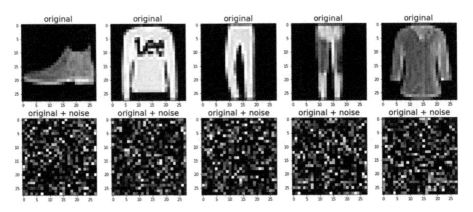

Figure 11-6. *Fashion MNIST Clean vs. Noisy Image Examples*

As you can see, we applied a heavy noise to our images, and no one can tell that there are apparel items in the images at the bottom. But, with our autoencoder, we will be able to denoise these extremely noisy images.

Building the Model

As we did in Chapter 10, we again make use of Model Subclassing. In Model Subclassing, we are free to implement everything from scratch. It is a very powerful method since we can build any type of model. Our custom class would extend `tf.keras.Model` object. It also requires declaring several variables and functions. However, it is nothing to be afraid of. To build a model, we simply need to complete the following tasks:

- Create a class extending the `keras.Model` object.

- Create an __init__ function to declare two separate models built with Sequential API.

    - Within them, we need to declare layers that would reverse each other. Conv2D layer for encoder model, whereas Conv2DTranspose layer for decoder model.

- Create a call function to tell the model how to process the inputs using the initialized variables with __init__ method:

    - We need to call the initialized encoder model which takes the images as input.

    - We also need to call the initialized decoder model which takes the output of the encoder model (encoded) as input.

- Return the output of the decoder.

The following code does all of them:

```
class Denoise(tf.keras.Model):
  def __init__(self):
    super(Denoise, self).__init__()
```

```python
self.encoder = tf.keras.Sequential([
  Input(shape=(28, 28, 1)),
  Conv2D(16, (3,3), activation='relu', padding='same',
  strides=2),
  Conv2D(8, (3,3), activation='relu', padding='same',
  strides=2)])

self.decoder = tf.keras.Sequential([
  Conv2DTranspose(8, kernel_size=3, strides=2,
   activation='relu', padding='same'),
  Conv2DTranspose(16, kernel_size=3, strides=2,
  activation='relu', padding='same'),
  Conv2D(1, kernel_size=(3,3), activation='sigmoid',
  padding='same')])

def call(self, x):
  encoded = self.encoder(x)
  decoded = self.decoder(encoded)
  return decoded
```

Let's create a model object with the following code:

```python
autoencoder = Denoise()
```

We use Adam optimizer as our optimization algorithm and mean squared error (MSE) as our loss function. The following code sets these configurations:

```python
autoencoder.compile(optimizer='adam', loss='mse')
```

Finally, we can run our model for 10 epochs by feeding the noisy and the clean images, which will take about 1 minute to train. We also use test datasets for validation. The following code is for training the model:

```python
autoencoder.fit(x_train_noisy, x_train,
```

Figure 11-7 shows the training process outputs for each epoch:

```
epochs=10,
shuffle=True,
validation_data=(x_test_noisy, x_test))
```

```
Epoch 1/10
1875/1875 [==============================] - 5s 3ms/step - loss: 0.0287 - val_loss: 0.1980
Epoch 2/10
1875/1875 [==============================] - 5s 3ms/step - loss: 0.0206 - val_loss: 0.1979
Epoch 3/10
1875/1875 [==============================] - 5s 3ms/step - loss: 0.0201 - val_loss: 0.1972
Epoch 4/10
1875/1875 [==============================] - 5s 3ms/step - loss: 0.0198 - val_loss: 0.1976
Epoch 5/10
1875/1875 [==============================] - 5s 3ms/step - loss: 0.0195 - val_loss: 0.1972
Epoch 6/10
1875/1875 [==============================] - 5s 3ms/step - loss: 0.0193 - val_loss: 0.1984
Epoch 7/10
1875/1875 [==============================] - 5s 3ms/step - loss: 0.0192 - val_loss: 0.1998
Epoch 8/10
1875/1875 [==============================] - 5s 3ms/step - loss: 0.0190 - val_loss: 0.1995
Epoch 9/10
1875/1875 [==============================] - 5s 3ms/step - loss: 0.0189 - val_loss: 0.1966
Epoch 10/10
1875/1875 [==============================] - 5s 3ms/step - loss: 0.0188 - val_loss: 0.1974
<tensorflow.python.keras.callbacks.History at 0x7f0ae8d77b00>
```

Figure 11-7. *The Epoch Stats During Our Custom Model Training*

Denoising Noisy Images

Now that we trained our model, we can easily do denoising tasks. For the simplicity of the prediction process, we use the test dataset. But, feel free to process and try other images such as digits in the MNIST dataset.

For now, we run the following lines to denoise the noisy test images:

```
encoded_imgs=autoencoder.encoder(x_test).numpy()
decoded_imgs=autoencoder.decoder(encoded_imgs.numpy()
```

As you can see here, we can use the encoder and the decoder networks separately with their corresponding attributes. Therefore, we first use the encoder network to encode our images (x_test). Then, we use these encoded images (encoded_imgs) in the decoder network to generate the clean versions (decoded_imgs) of the images that we used in the beginning.

We can compare the noisy, reconstructed (denoised), and original versions of the first ten images of the test dataset with the following code:

```
n = 10
plt.figure(figsize=(20, 6))
for i in range(n):
    # display original + noise
    bx = plt.subplot(3, n, i + 1)
    plt.title("original + noise")
    plt.imshow(tf.squeeze(x_test_noisy[i]))
    plt.gray()
    ax.get_xaxis().set_visible(False)
    ax.get_yaxis().set_visible(False)

    # display reconstruction
    cx = plt.subplot(3, n, i + n + 1)
    plt.title("reconstructed")
    plt.imshow(tf.squeeze(decoded_imgs[i]))
    plt.gray()
    bx.get_xaxis().set_visible(False)
    bx.get_yaxis().set_visible(False)

    # display original
    ax = plt.subplot(3, n, i + 2*n + 1)
    plt.title("original")
    plt.imshow(tf.squeeze(x_test[i]))
    plt.gray()
    ax.get_xaxis().set_visible(False)
    ax.get_yaxis().set_visible(False)
plt.show()
```

Figure 11-8 shows the noisy, reconstructed, and original versions of selected images:

Output:

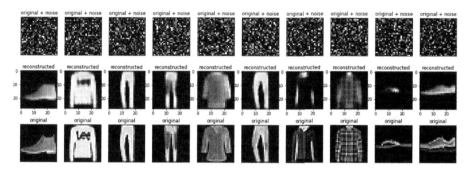

Figure 11-8. *Fashion MNIST Test Dataset Sample Images with Noisy, Reconstructed (Denoised), and Original Versions*

As you can see previously, our model can successfully denoise very noisy photos, which it has never seen before (we used the test dataset). There are obviously some non-recovered distortions, such as the missing bottom of the slippers in the second image from the right. Yet, if you consider how deformed the noisy images, we can say that our model is pretty successful in recovering the distorted images.

Off the top of my head, you can – for instance – consider extending this autoencoder and embed it into a photo enhancement app, which can increase the clarity and crispiness of the photos.

Conclusion

In this chapter, we covered a neural network architecture, autoencoders, which are mainly used for unsupervised learning tasks. We also conducted a case study, in which we trained an autoencoder model which is capable of denoising distorted images.

In the next chapter, we will dive into the generative adversarial networks, which revolutionize the generative side of deep learning.

CHAPTER 12

Generative Adversarial Network

Generative adversarial networks (GANs) are a type of deep learning model designed by Ian Goodfellow and his colleagues in 2014.

The invention of GANs has occurred pretty unexpectedly. The famous researcher, then, a PhD fellow at the University of Montreal, Ian Goodfellow, landed on the idea when he was discussing with his friends – at a friend's going away party – about the flaws of the other generative algorithms. After the party, he came home with high hopes and implemented the concept he had in mind. Surprisingly, everything went as he hoped in the first trial, and he successfully created the generative adversarial networks (shortly, GANs).

According to Yann LeCun, the director of AI research at Facebook and a professor at New York University, GANs are *"the most interesting idea in the last 10 years in machine learning."*

Method

In a GAN architecture, there are two neural networks (a generator and a discriminator) competing with each other in a game. After being exposed to a training set, the generator learns to generate new samples with similar characteristics. The discriminator, on the other hand, tries to figure out

© Orhan Gazi Yalçın 2021
O. G. Yalçın, *Applied Neural Networks with TensorFlow 2*,
https://doi.org/10.1007/978-1-4842-6513-0_12

if the generated data is authentic or manufactured. Through training, the generator is forced to generate near-authentic samples so that the discriminator cannot differentiate them from the training data. After this training, we can use the generator to generate very realistic samples such as images, sounds, and text.

GANs are initially designed to address unsupervised learning tasks. However, recent studies showed that GANs show promising results in supervised, semi-supervised, and reinforcement learning tasks as well.

Architecture

As mentioned earlier, there are two networks forming a generative adversarial network: a generator network and a discriminator network. These two networks are connected to each other with a latent space where all the magic happens. In other words, we use the output of the generator network as the input in the discriminator network. Let's take an in-depth look at the generative and discriminative networks to truly understand how GANs function; see Figure 12-1:

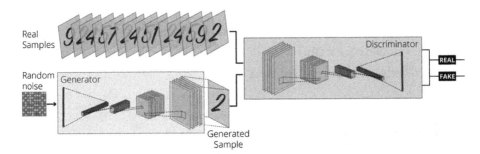

Figure 12-1. *A Visualization of a Generative Adversarial Network*

GAN Components

Generative Network

A generator network takes a fixed-length random vector (starting with random noise) and generates a new sample. It uses a Gaussian distribution to generate new samples and usually starts with a one-dimensional layer, which is reshaped into the shape of the training data samples in the end. For example, if we use the MNIST dataset to generate images, the output layer of the generator network must correspond to the image dimensions (e.g., 28 x 28 x 1). This final layer is also referred to as latent space or vector space.

Discriminator Network

A discriminator network works in a relatively reversed order. The output of the generative network is used as input data in the discriminator network (e.g., 28 x 28 x 1). The main task of a discriminator network is to decide if the generated sample is authentic or not. Therefore, the output of a discriminator network is provided by a single neuron dense layer outputting the probability (e.g., 0.6475) of the authenticity of the generated sample.

Latent Space

Latent space (i.e.,vector space) functions as the generator network's output and the discriminator network's input. The latent space in a generative adversarial model usually has the shape of the original training dataset samples. Latent Space tries to catch the characteristic features of the training dataset so that the generator may successfully generate close to authentic samples.

A Known Issue: Mode Collapse

During the training of the generative adversarial networks, we often encounter with the "mode collapse" issue. Mode collapse basically refers to the failure to generalize correctly or, in other words, failure to learn the meaningful characteristics for successful sample generation. Mode collapse may be in the form of failure to learn altogether or failure to learn partial features. For example, when we work with the MNIST dataset (handwritten digits from 0 to 9), due to mode collapse issue, our GAN may never learn to generate some of the digits. There are two potential explanations for mode collapse:

- Weak discriminative network

- Wrong choice of objective function

Therefore, playing around with the size and depth of our network, as well as with objective function, may fix the issue.

Final Notes on Architecture

It is essential to maintain healthy competition between generator and discriminator networks to build useful GAN models. As long as these two networks work against each other to perfect their performances, you can freely design the internal structure of these networks, depending on the problem. For example, when you are dealing with sequence data, you can build two networks with LSTM and GRU layers as long as one of them acts as a generator network, whereas the other acts as a discriminator network. Another example would be our case study. When to generate images with GANS, we add our networks a number of Convolution or Transposed Convolution layers since they decrease the computational complexity of the image data.

Applications of GANs

There are a number of areas where the GANs are currently in use which may be listed as follows:

- Fashion, art, and advertising

- Manufacturing and R&D

- Video games

- Malicious applications and deep fake

- Other applications

Art and Fashion

Generative adversarial networks are capable of "generating" samples. So, they are inherently creative. That's why one of the most promising fields for generative adversarial networks is art and fashion. With well-trained GANs, you can generate paintings, songs, apparels, and even poems. In fact, a painting generated by Nvidia's StyleGAN network, "Edmond de Belamy, from La Famille de Belamy," was sold in New York for $432,500. Therefore, you may clearly see how GAN has the potential to be used in the art world.

Manufacturing, Research, and R&D

GANs can be used to predict computational bottlenecks in scientific research projects as well as in industrial applications.

GAN networks can also be used to increase the definition of images based on statistical distributions. In other words, GANs can predict the missing pieces using statistical distributions and generate suitable pixel values, which would increase the quality of the images taken by telescopes or microscopes.

Video Games

GANs may be used to obtain more precise and sharper images using small definition images. This ability may be used to make old games more appealing to new generations.

Malicious Applications and Deep Fake

GANs may be used to generate close-to-authentic fake social profiles or fake videos of celebrities. For example, a GAN algorithm may be used to fabricate fake evidence to frame someone. Therefore, there are a number of malicious GAN applications and also a number of GANs to detect the samples generated by the malicious GANs and label them as fake.

Miscellaneous Applications

Apart from the preceding use cases, GANs are used with the following purposes:

- For early diagnosis in the medical industry
- To generate photorealistic images in architecture and internal design industries
- To reconstruct three-dimensional models of objects from images
- For image manipulation such as aging
- To generate protein sequences which may be used in cancer studies
- To reconstruct a person's face by using their voice.

The generative adversarial network applications are vast and limitless, and it is a very hot topic in the artificial intelligence community. Now that we covered the basics of generative adversarial networks, we can start working on our case study. Note that we will do our own take from deep convolutional GAN tutorial released by the TensorFlow team.[1]

Case Study I Digit Generation with MNIST

In this case study, step by step, we build a generative adversarial network (GAN), which is capable of generating handwritten digits (0 to 9). To be able to complete this task, we need to build a generator network as well as a discriminator network so that our generative model can learn to trick the discriminator model, which inspects what the generator network manufactures. Let's start with our initial imports.

Initial Imports

As we always do in our case studies, we make some initial imports, which are used throughout different cells of our Colab notebook. The following lines import TensorFlow, relevant TensorFlow layer objects, and Matplotlib:

```
import tensorflow as tf
from tensorflow.keras.layers import(Dense,
                          BatchNormalization,
                          LeakyReLU,
                          Reshape,
                          Conv2DTranspose,
                          Conv2D,
                          Dropout,
                          Flatten)
import matplotlib.pyplot as plt
```

---

[1]Deep Convolutional Generative Adversarial Network, TensorFlow, available at www.tensorflow.org/tutorials/generative/dcgan

In the upcoming parts, we also use other libraries such as *os, time, IPython.display, PIL, glob, and imageio,* but to keep them relevant with the context, we only import them when we will use them.

Load and Process the MNIST Dataset

We already covered the details of the MNIST dataset a few times. It is a dataset of handwritten digits with 60,000 training and 10,000 test samples. If you want to know more about the MNIST dataset, please refer to Chapter 7.

Since this is an unsupervised learning task, we only need the features, and therefore we don't save the label arrays. Let's import the dataset with the following lines:

```
# underscore to omit the label arrays
(train_images, train_labels), (_, _) = tf.keras.datasets.mnist.
load_data()
```

Then, we reshape our train_images to have a fourth dimension and normalize it (in range of -1 to 1) with the following code:

```
train_images = train_images.reshape(train_images.shape[0], 28,
28, 1).astype('float32')
train_images = (train_images - 127.5) / 127.5 # Normalize the
images to [-1, 1]
```

Then, we set a BUFFER_SIZE for shuffling and a BATCH_SIZE for processing the data in batches. Then, we call the following function to convert our NumPy array into a TensorFlow Dataset object:

```
# Batch and shuffle the data
train_dataset = tf.data.Dataset.from_tensor_slices(train_
images).shuffle(BUFFER_SIZE).batch(BATCH_SIZE)
```

Now our data is processed and cleaned. We can move on to the model-building part.

Build the GAN Model

As opposed to the other case studies, the model-building part of this case study is slightly more advanced. We need to define custom loss, training step, and training loop functions. It may be a bit more challenging to grasp what is happening. But I try to add as much comment as possible to make it easier for you. Also, consider this case study as a path to becoming an advanced machine learning expert. Besides, if you really pay attention to the comments, it is much easier than how it looks.

Generator Network

As part of our GAN network, we first build a generator with Sequential API. The generator would accept a one-dimensional input with 100 data points and slowly converts it into an image data of 28 x 28 pixels. Since we use this model to generate images from one-dimensional input, using Transposed Convolution layers is the best option. Transposed Convolution layers work just the opposite of the Convolution layer. They increase the definition of image data. We also take advantage of Batch Normalization and Leaky ReLU layers after using Transposed Convolution layers. The following code defines this network for us:

```
def make_generator_model():
  model = tf.keras.Sequential()
  model.add(Dense(7*7*256, use_bias=False, input_shape=(100,)))
  model.add(BatchNormalization())
  model.add(LeakyReLU())

  model.add(Reshape((7, 7, 256)))
  assert model.output_shape == (None, 7, 7, 256) # Note: None
is the batch size

  model.add(Conv2DTranspose(128, (5, 5), strides=(1, 1),
padding="same", use_bias=False))
```

```
assert model.output_shape == (None, 7, 7, 128)
model.add(BatchNormalization())
model.add(LeakyReLU())

model.add(Conv2DTranspose(64, (5, 5), strides=(2, 2),
padding="same", use_bias=False))
assert model.output_shape == (None, 14, 14, 64)
model.add(BatchNormalization())
model.add(LeakyReLU())

model.add(Conv2DTranspose(1, (5, 5), strides=(2, 2),
padding="same", use_bias=False, activation="tanh"))
assert model.output_shape == (None, 28, 28, 1)

return model
```

We can declare our network with the following code:

```
generator = make_generator_model()
```

Let's take a look at the summary of our generator network in Figure 12-2:

```
generator.summary()
Output:
```

```
Model: "sequential"
```

Layer (type)	Output Shape	Param #
dense (Dense)	(None, 12544)	1254400
batch_normalization (BatchNo	(None, 12544)	50176
leaky_re_lu (LeakyReLU)	(None, 12544)	0
reshape (Reshape)	(None, 7, 7, 256)	0
conv2d_transpose (Conv2DTran	(None, 7, 7, 128)	819200
batch_normalization_1 (Batch	(None, 7, 7, 128)	512
leaky_re_lu_1 (LeakyReLU)	(None, 7, 7, 128)	0
conv2d_transpose_1 (Conv2DTr	(None, 14, 14, 64)	204800
batch_normalization_2 (Batch	(None, 14, 14, 64)	256
leaky_re_lu_2 (LeakyReLU)	(None, 14, 14, 64)	0
conv2d_transpose_2 (Conv2DTr	(None, 28, 28, 1)	1600

```
Total params: 2,330,944
Trainable params: 2,305,472
Non-trainable params: 25,472
```

Figure 12-2. *The Summary of Our Generator Network*

And generate and plot a sample using our untrained generator network with the following code:

```
# Create a random noise and generate a sample
noise = tf.random.normal([1, 100])
generated_image = generator(noise, training=False)
# Visualize the generated sample
plt.imshow(generated_image[0, :, :, 0], cmap="gray")
Output is shown in Figure 12-3:
```

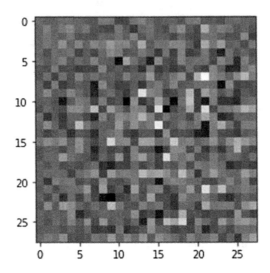

Figure 12-3. *An Example of the Randomly Generated Sample Without Training*

Discriminator Network

After the generator network, we should build a discriminator network to inspect the samples generated by the generator. Our discriminator network must decide on the probability of the fakeness of the generated images. Therefore, it takes the generated image data (28 x 28) and outputs a single value. For this task, we use Convolution layers supported by Leaky ReLU and Dropout layers. Flatten layers convert two-dimensional data into one-dimensional data, and Dense layer is used to convert the output into a single value. The following lines define the function for our discriminator network:

```
def make_discriminator_model():
    model = tf.keras.Sequential()
```

```
  model.add(Conv2D(64, (5, 5), strides=(2, 2), padding="same",
input_shape=[28, 28, 1]))
  model.add(LeakyReLU())
  model.add(Dropout(0.3))

  model.add(Conv2D(128, (5, 5), strides=(2, 2),
padding="same"))
  model.add(LeakyReLU())
  model.add(Dropout(0.3))

  model.add(Flatten())
  model.add(Dense(1))

  return model
```

We can create the discriminator network by calling the function:

```
discriminator = make_discriminator_model()
```

And we can see the summary of our discriminator network with the following code (see Figure 12-4 for the output):

```
discriminator.summary()
```
Output:

```
Model: "sequential_1"
```

Layer (type)	Output Shape	Param #
conv2d (Conv2D)	(None, 14, 14, 64)	1664
leaky_re_lu_3 (LeakyReLU)	(None, 14, 14, 64)	0
dropout (Dropout)	(None, 14, 14, 64)	0
conv2d_1 (Conv2D)	(None, 7, 7, 128)	204928
leaky_re_lu_4 (LeakyReLU)	(None, 7, 7, 128)	0
dropout_1 (Dropout)	(None, 7, 7, 128)	0
flatten (Flatten)	(None, 6272)	0
dense_1 (Dense)	(None, 1)	6273

```
Total params: 212,865
Trainable params: 212,865
Non-trainable params: 0
```

Figure 12-4. *The Summary of Our Discriminator Network*

If we use the discriminator network, we can actually decide if our randomly generated image is authentic enough or not:

```
decision = discriminator(generated_image)
print (decision)
```
Output:
```
tf.Tensor([[-0.00108097]], shape=(1, 1), dtype=float32)
```

As you can see, our output is less than zero, and we can conclude that this particular sample generated by the untrained generator network is fake.

Configure the GAN Network

As part of our model configuration, we need to set loss functions for both the generator and the discriminator. In addition, we need to set separate optimizers for both of them as well.

Loss Function

We start by creating a Binary Crossentropy object from tf.keras.losses module. We also set from_logits parameter to true. After creating the object, we fill them with custom discriminator and generator loss functions.

Our discriminator loss is calculated as a combination of (i) the discriminator's predictions on real images to an array of ones and (ii) its predictions on generated images to an array of zeros.

Our generator loss is calculated by measuring how well it was able to trick the discriminator. Therefore, we need to compare the discriminator's decisions on the generated images to an array of ones.

The following lines do all of these:

```
# This method returns a helper function to compute cross
entropy loss
cross_entropy = tf.keras.losses.BinaryCrossentropy(from_
logits=True)

def discriminator_loss(real_output, fake_output):
  real_loss = cross_entropy(tf.ones_like(real_output), real_
  output)
  fake_loss = cross_entropy(tf.zeros_like(fake_output), fake_
  output)
  total_loss = real_loss + fake_loss
  return total_loss

def generator_loss(fake_output):
  return cross_entropy(tf.ones_like(fake_output), fake_output)
```

Optimizer

We also set two optimizers separately for generator and discriminator networks. We can use the Adam object from `tf.keras.optimizers` module. The following lines set the optimizers:

```
generator_optimizer=tf.keras.optimizers.Adam(1e-4)
discriminator_optimizer=tf.keras.optimizers.Adam(1e-4)
```

Set the Checkpoint

Training the GAN network takes longer than other networks due to the complexity of the network. We have to run the training for at least 50–60 epochs to generate meaningful images. Therefore, setting checkpoints is very useful to use our model later on.

By using the os library, we set a path to save all the training steps with the following lines:

```
import os

checkpoint_dir = './training_checkpoints'

checkpoint_prefix=os.path.join(checkpoint_dir, "ckpt")

checkpoint = tf.train.Checkpoint(
  generator_optimizer=generator_optimizer,
  discriminator_optimizer=discriminator_optimizer,
  generator=generator,
  discriminator=discriminator)
```

Train the GAN Model

Let's create some of the variables with the following lines:

```
EPOCHS = 60
# We will reuse this seed overtime (so it's easier)
# to visualize progress in the animated GIF)
noise_dim = 100
num_examples_to_generate = 16
seed = tf.random.normal([num_examples_to_generate, noise_dim])
```

Our seed is the noise that we use to generate images on top of. The following code generates a random array with normal distribution with the shape (16, 100).

The Training Step

This is the most unusual part of our model: We are setting a custom training step. After defining the custom train_step() function by annotating the tf.function module, our model will be trained based on the custom train_step() function we defined.

The following code with excessive comments are for the training step. Please read the comments carefully.

```
# tf.function annotation causes the function
# to be "compiled" as part of the training
@tf.function
def train_step(images):
  # 1 - Create a random noise to feed it into the model
  # for the image generation
  noise = tf.random.normal([BATCH_SIZE, noise_dim])
  # 2 - Generate images and calculate loss values
  # GradientTape method records operations for automatic
  differentiation.
```

```
  with tf.GradientTape() as gen_tape, tf.GradientTape() as
disc_tape:
    generated_images = generator(noise, training=True)
    real_output = discriminator(images, training=True)
    fake_output = discriminator(generated_images,
training=True)
    gen_loss = generator_loss(fake_output)
    disc_loss = discriminator_loss(real_output, fake_output)

  # 3 - Calculate gradients using loss values and model
variables
  # "gradient" method computes the gradient using
  # operations recorded in context of this tape (gen_tape and
disc_tape).
  # It accepts a target (e.g., gen_loss) variable and
  # a source variable (e.g.,generator.trainable_variables)
  # target --> a list or nested structure of Tensors or
Variables to be differentiated.
  # source --> a list or nested structure of Tensors or
Variables.
  # target will be differentiated against elements in sources.
  # "gradient" method returns a list or nested structure of Tensors
  # (or IndexedSlices, or None), one for each element in
sources.
  # Returned structure is the same as the structure of sources.
  gradients_of_generator = gen_tape.gradient(gen_loss,
generator.trainable_variables)
  gradients_of_discriminator = disc_tape.gradient( disc_loss,
discriminator.trainable_variables)
  # 4 - Process  Gradients and Run the Optimizer
  # "apply_gradients" method processes aggregated gradients.
  # ex: optimizer.apply_gradients(zip(grads, vars))
  """
```

276

```
Example use of apply_gradients:
grads = tape.gradient(loss, vars)
grads = tf.distribute.get_replica_context().all_reduce('sum',
grads)
# Processing aggregated gradients.
optimizer.apply_gradients(zip(grads, vars), experimental_
aggregate_gradients=False)
"""
generator_optimizer.apply_gradients(zip( gradients_of_
generator, generator.trainable_variables))
discriminator_optimizer.apply_gradients(zip( gradients_of_
discriminator, discriminator.trainable_variables))
```

Now that we defined our custom training step with `tf.function` annotation, we can define our train function for the training loop.

The Training Loop

We define a function, named `train`, for our training loop. Not only we run a for loop to iterate our custom training step over the MNIST, but also do the following with a single function:

- During the training
  - Start recording time spent at the beginning of each epoch
  - Produce GIF images and display them
  - Save the model every 5 epochs as a checkpoint
  - Print out the completed epoch time
- Generate a final image in the end after the training is completed

277

The following lines with detailed comments do all these tasks:

```python
import time
from IPython import display # A command shell for interactive
computing in Python.

def train(dataset, epochs):
  # A. For each epoch, do the following:
  for epoch in range(epochs):
  start = time.time()
  # 1 - For each batch of the epoch,
  for image_batch in dataset:
    # 1.a - run the custom "train_step" function
    # we just declared above
    train_step(image_batch)

  # 2 - Produce images for the GIF as we go
  display.clear_output(wait=True)
  generate_and_save_images(generator,
                           epoch + 1,
                           seed)

  # 3 - Save the model every 5 epochs as
  # a checkpoint, which we will use later
  if (epoch + 1) % 5 == 0:
    checkpoint.save(file_prefix = checkpoint_prefix)

  # 4 - Print out the completed epoch no. and the time spent
  print ('Time for epoch {} is {} sec'.format(epoch + 1, time.
time()-start))

  # B. Generate a final image after the training is completed
  display.clear_output(wait=True)
  generate_and_save_images(generator,
                           epochs,
                           seed)
```

Image Generation Function

In the train function, there is a custom image generation function that we haven't defined yet. Our image generation function does the following tasks:

- Generate images by using the model.

- Display the generated images in a 4 x 4 grid layout using Matplotlib.

- Save the final figure in the end.

The following lines are in charge of these tasks:

```python
def generate_and_save_images(model, epoch, test_input):
  # Notice `training` is set to False.
  # This is so all layers run in inference mode (batchnorm).
  # 1 - Generate images
  predictions = model(test_input, training=False)
  # 2 - Plot the generated images
  fig = plt.figure(figsize=(4,4))
  for i in range(predictions.shape[0]):
    plt.subplot(4, 4, i+1)
    plt.imshow(predictions[i, :, :, 0] * 127.5 + 127.5,
cmap="gray")
      plt.axis('off')

  # 3 - Save the generated images

  plt.savefig('image_at_epoch_{:04d}.png'.format( epoch))
  plt.show()
```

Now that we defined our custom image generation function, we can safely call our train function in the next part.

Start the Training

Starting the training loop is very easy. The single line of the following code would start training with the train function, which loops over the `train_step()` function and generates images using `generate_and_save_images()` function. We also receive stats and info during the process, as well as the generated images on a 4 x 4 grid layout.

```
train(train_dataset, EPOCHS)
```
Output:

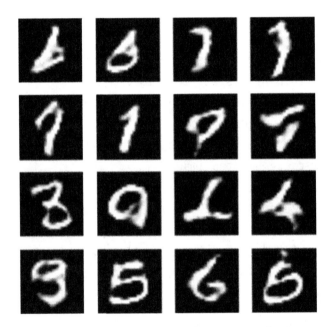

Figure 12-5. The Generated Images After 60 Epochs in 4 x 4 Grid Layout

As you can see in Figure 12-5, after 60 epochs, the generated images are very close to proper handwritten digits. The only digit I cannot spot is the digit two (2), which could just be a coincidence.

CHAPTER 12   GENERATIVE ADVERSARIAL NETWORK

Now that we trained our model and saved our checkpoints, we can restore the trained model with the following line:

```
checkpoint.restore(tf.train.latest_checkpoint(checkpoint_dir))
```

Animate Generated Digits During the Training

During the training, our generate_and_save_images() function successfully saved a 4 x 4 generated image grid layout at each epoch. Let's see how our model's generative abilities evolve over time with a simple exercise.

To be able to open the images, we can use PIL (Python Image Library), which supports many different image formats, including PNG. We can define a custom function to open images with the following lines:

```
# PIL is a library which may open different image file formats
import PIL
# Display a single image using the epoch number
def display_image(epoch_no):
  return PIL.Image.open( 'image_at_epoch_{:04d}.png'.format(
epoch_no ))
Now test the function with the following line, which would
display the latest PNG file generated by our model:

display_image(EPOCHS)
```
Output is shown in Figure 12-6:

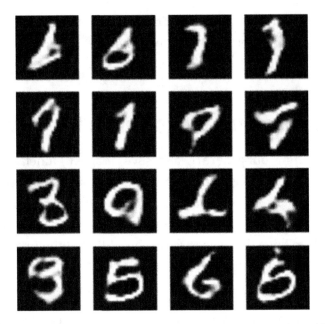

Figure 12-6. *The Display of the Latest PNG File Generated by the GAN Model. Note That They Are Identical to Samples Shown in Figure 12-5. Since We Restored the Model from the Last Checkpoint*

With `display_images()` function, we may display any image we want. On top of this option, wouldn't it be cool to generate an animated GIF image showing how our model evolved over time? We can achieve this using glob and imageio libraries, which would pile up all the PNG files to create an animated GIF file. The following lines do this task:

```
import glob # The glob module is used for Unix style pathname
pattern expansion.
import imageio # The library that provides an easy interface to
read and write a wide range of image data

anim_file = 'dcgan.gif'
```

```
with imageio.get_writer(anim_file, mode="I") as writer:
  filenames = glob.glob('image*.png')
  filenames = sorted(filenames)
  for filename in filenames:
    image = imageio.imread(filename)
    writer.append_data(image)
  image = imageio.imread(filename)
  writer.append_data(image)
```

Click the *Files* icon on the left side of your Google Colab Notebook to view all the files, including '*dcgan.gif*.' You can simply download it to view an animated version of the images our model generated at each epoch. To be able to view the GIF image within your Google Colab Notebook, you can use the following line:

```
display.Image(open('dcgan.gif','rb').read())
```

Figure 12-7 shows several frames from the GIF image we created:

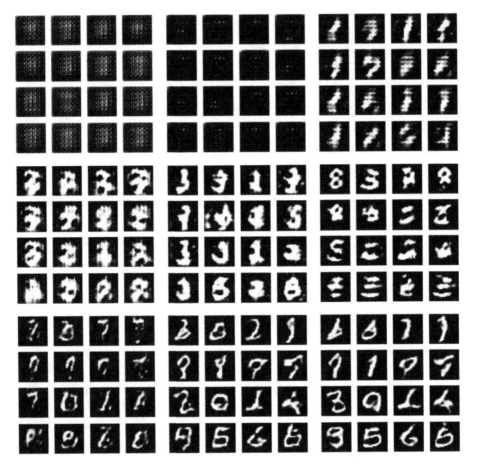

Figure 12-7. *Generated Digit Examples from the Different Epochs.*
See How the GAN Model Learns to Generate Digits Over Time

Conclusion

In this chapter, we covered our last neural network architecture, generative adversarial networks, which are mainly used for generative tasks in fields such as art, manufacturing, research, and gaming. We also conducted a case study, in which we trained a GAN model which is capable of generating handwritten digits.

Index

A

© Orhan Gazi Yalçın 2021
O. G. Yalçın, *Applied Neural Networks with TensorFlow 2*,
https://doi.org/10.1007/978-1-4842-6513-0

Printed in the United States
By Bookmasters